PROTECTING NORTH KOREAN REFUGEES

HEARING

BEFORE THE

SUBCOMMITTEE ON AFRICA, GLOBAL HEALTH, GLOBAL HUMAN RIGHTS, AND INTERNATIONAL ORGANIZATIONS

OF THE

COMMITTEE ON FOREIGN AFFAIRS
HOUSE OF REPRESENTATIVES

ONE HUNDRED FIFTEENTH CONGRESS

FIRST SESSION

DECEMBER 12, 2017

Serial No. 115–98

Printed for the use of the Committee on Foreign Affairs

Available via the World Wide Web: http://www.foreignaffairs.house.gov/ or
http://www.gpo.gov/fdsys/

U.S. GOVERNMENT PUBLISHING OFFICE

27–811PDF   WASHINGTON : 2018

For sale by the Superintendent of Documents, U.S. Government Publishing Office
Internet: bookstore.gpo.gov   Phone: toll free (866) 512–1800; DC area (202) 512–1800
Fax: (202) 512–2104   Mail: Stop IDCC, Washington, DC 20402–0001

COMMITTEE ON FOREIGN AFFAIRS

EDWARD R. ROYCE, California, *Chairman*

CHRISTOPHER H. SMITH, New Jersey	ELIOT L. ENGEL, New York
ILEANA ROS-LEHTINEN, Florida	BRAD SHERMAN, California
DANA ROHRABACHER, California	GREGORY W. MEEKS, New York
STEVE CHABOT, Ohio	ALBIO SIRES, New Jersey
JOE WILSON, South Carolina	GERALD E. CONNOLLY, Virginia
MICHAEL T. McCAUL, Texas	THEODORE E. DEUTCH, Florida
TED POE, Texas	KAREN BASS, California
DARRELL E. ISSA, California	WILLIAM R. KEATING, Massachusetts
TOM MARINO, Pennsylvania	DAVID N. CICILLINE, Rhode Island
MO BROOKS, Alabama PAUL	AMI BERA, California
COOK, California SCOTT	LOIS FRANKEL, Florida
PERRY, Pennsylvania RON	TULSI GABBARD, Hawaii
DeSANTIS, Florida	JOAQUIN CASTRO, Texas
MARK MEADOWS, North Carolina	ROBIN L. KELLY, Illinois
TED S. YOHO, Florida	BRENDAN F. BOYLE, Pennsylvania
ADAM KINZINGER, Illinois	DINA TITUS, Nevada
LEE M. ZELDIN, New York	NORMA J. TORRES, California
DANIEL M. DONOVAN, JR., New York	BRADLEY SCOTT SCHNEIDER, Illinois
F. JAMES SENSENBRENNER, JR.,	THOMAS R. SUOZZI, New York
Wisconsin	ADRIANO ESPAILLAT, New York
ANN WAGNER, Missouri	TED LIEU, California
BRIAN J. MAST, Florida	
FRANCIS ROONEY, Florida	
BRIAN K. FITZPATRICK, Pennsylvania	
THOMAS A. GARRETT, JR., Virginia	
JOHN R. CURTIS, Utah	

AMY PORTER, *Chief of Staff*   THOMAS SHEEHY, *Staff Director*
JASON STEINBAUM, *Democratic Staff Director*

———

SUBCOMMITTEE ON AFRICA, GLOBAL HEALTH, GLOBAL HUMAN RIGHTS, AND
INTERNATIONAL ORGANIZATIONS

CHRISTOPHER H. SMITH, New Jersey, *Chairman*

MARK MEADOWS, North Carolina	KAREN BASS, California
DANIEL M. DONOVAN, JR., New York	AMI BERA, California
F. JAMES SENSENBRENNER, JR.,	JOAQUIN CASTRO, Texas
Wisconsin	THOMAS R. SUOZZI, New York
THOMAS A. GARRETT, JR., Virginia	

CONTENTS

Page

WITNESSES

LETTERS, STATEMENTS, ETC., SUBMITTED FOR THE HEARING

APPENDIX

PROTECTING NORTH KOREAN REFUGEES

TUESDAY, DECEMBER 12, 2017

House of Representatives,
Subcommittee on Africa, Global Health,
Global Human Rights, and International Organizations,
Committee on Foreign Affairs,
Washington, DC.

The subcommittee met, pursuant to notice, at 2:00 p.m., in room 2200 Rayburn House Office Building, Hon. Christopher H. Smith (chairman of the subcommittee) presiding.

Mr. SMITH. The subcommittee will come to order, and good afternoon to everybody.

At a recent House Foreign Affairs Committee hearing, North Korea defector Ambassador Thae Yong-Ho testified about the strategic value of both disseminating information into North Korea and the protection of North Korean refugees in China.

Drawing on an analogy about the fall of the Berlin Wall, Ambassador Thae claimed that there may be a similar result if China stopped repatriations of refugees in the United States and the international community, expanded soft power news and information flows into North Korea.

He was very dramatic in his testimony and couldn't be clearer just how much of a game changer it would be if the refugees could find a place of refuge in China, and then on to other places like South Korea and other places where freedom flourishes.

This hearing will explore the current situation facing North Korean asylum seekers and assess both the Chinese legal obligation to protect refugees and the effectiveness of global efforts to stop what the U.N. Commission on Inquiry on Human Rights in North Korea called crimes against humanity experienced by refugees.

As the Congress continues to look at ways to best apply maximum diplomatic and financial pressure on the regime of Kim Jong-un, this hearing will explore the strategic relevance of further pressing the Chinese Government to protect North Korean refugees and evaluate the impact of surging outside information into North Korea will have.

Amid escalating tensions on the Korean Peninsula, we cannot forget those suffering under the North Korean regime and those North Korean refugees who are in China.

North Korean asylum seekers are in imminent risk of repatriation, torture, sexual violence, forced abortions, hard labor, and even execution.

China's repatriations of the North Koreans is a stark violation of both the spirit and the letter of the Refugee Convention and the 1967 protocol to which China has acceded.

The Chinese Government has a lot to answer for. It is no wonder that the U.N. Commission on Inquiry for North Korea Human Rights concluded that the Government of the People's Republic of China is aiding and abetting in crimes against humanity by forcefully repatriating North Korean refugees.

I would note that as many as 90 percent of North Korean women refugees in China today fall prey to traffickers who will sell the refugees into sexual slavery or forced marriages.

Suzanne Scholte, who will testify during this hearing, previously brought women who were refugees from North Korea—Mrs. Ma and others—who for the first time told the story about how they were exploited inside of China and forced into sex trafficking.

It was just horrific testimony, but an eye opener about how they went from an exploitation in North Korea into exploitation into China.

Labor trafficking is also pervasive. The Government of North Korea and the government and businesses in China, Russia, and elsewhere in the world profit from the trafficking of North Korean laborers.

In recent months, Chinese authorities reportedly deported hundreds of South Korean missionaries and NGO workers who have provided crucial help to the North Korean refugees in China.

The people providing that assistance have been ousted as well. The international community, especially the United Nations, Trump administration, and the U.S. Congress must insist that China honor its treaty obligations and end its egregious practice of systematic repatriation of North Korean refugees.

I would note parenthetically I have raised this repeatedly with now the Secretary General and the former head of the UNHCR and never got a good answer. So the U.N. really needs to step up to the plate here.

Chinese officials and businesses complicit in repatriation of North Korean refugees or those who profit from labor trafficking should also be held accountable.

The Congress has given the administration the sanction tools that, if used, would send the right message and especially hold people to account. Whether it be through the North Korean Sanctions Enforcement Act, the Global Magnitsky Act, or those sanctions attached to China's Tier 3 designation for trafficking in persons.

All should be used strategically and swiftly to send a clear message. For too long the world has tolerated China's failures to protect refugees, and those complicit in repatriations of refugees who profit from the trafficking of North Koreans should be held accountable.

The annual repatriation should be a bellwether for judging China's willingness to curtail Kim Jong-un's nuclear ambitions. In addition to the protection of North Korean refugees, this hearing will also assess global efforts to surge news and information into North Korea.

Expansion of existing efforts to disseminate information into North Korea is especially important, if for nothing else than to tarnish and undermine the Kim family cult of personality where they are lifted up as gods.

The Kim family cult must be taken seriously as a national security threat and a barometer of Kim Jong-un's power. The cult of personality, sometimes called Juche, has inspired devotion from the North Korean people because of the cradle to grave propaganda that they endure.

We must undermine the Kim family cult and the big lies upon which it is based and the propaganda that grants Kim Jong-un almost godlike status.

This status has allowed three generations of the Kim family to starve and abuse the North Korean people and divert scarce resources to the military and to their nuclear programs.

We must have an information surge into North Korea. Human rights groups are smuggling DVDs and USB sticks with video about the Kim family's sins into North Korea right now.

Balloons are launched across the border with promises of a better life in South Korea. Radio programs broadcast daily messages and news urging North Korea's elite to defect and turn against Kim Jong-un.

We know some of these efforts are having an effect. We saw several high-level defections of diplomats, military officers, and the families of North Korea's elites in the last year alone.

The number of asylum seekers depressed for several years by upgraded security efforts in China have begun to rise. Efforts to get information into North Korea must be expanded dramatically and Washington should be leading this effort, working primarily with North Korean defector groups in South Korea and other human rights organizations.

The North Korean defector groups should be front and center in this effort. They know North Korea and they know the minds of the people. They know what information is needed to permanently tarnish the Kim family cult and what will motivate military leaders to defect.

Today's hearing takes place among growing tensions on the Korean Peninsula. We must seek all available options to deal with and resolve the issues at hand.

I now yield to my good friend and colleague, Ms. Bass, for any comments she might have.

Ms. BASS. As always, thank you, Mr. Chair, for your leadership on this issue and so many other issues, particularly involving human rights.

We know that this is an important hearing on the plight of refugees fleeing North Korea and the leadership role that we can play in protecting their human rights.

I also want to thank our witnesses for being here today and I look forward to your insight. I would especially like to thank them for their courage and their resolve to testify.

We know that North Korea is home to one of the most repressive governments in the world. The U.N. Commission on Inquiry on Human Rights has called for an investigation into violations that may amount to crimes against humanity, and it is common knowledge that the quality of life for everyday North Koreans is deplor-

4

able. They face widespread malnutrition, acute food shortages, and extreme poverty.

When it comes to these human rights abuses, Democrats and Republicans agree that the atrocities taking place in North Korea must be stopped.

We must continue to pursue bipartisan policies that promote human rights and work with the U.N. and our international partners to hold North Korea accountable.

While our military options in North Korea area limited, we can still advance human rights and respect the aspirations of the people there.

One way to do so is through information. North Koreans have limited knowledge of the outside world but increasing their access to information can help create an informed populace which will in turn benefit them as well as the international community.

I would like to point out that although the number of North Koreans seeking asylum in the U.S. is low, it behooves us to welcome and support those refugees who do reach us, given how much they have already suffered.

The people attempting to escape North Korea face insurmountable odds, mostly to China where they are likely to be repatriated to North Korean officials and forced in the labor camps.

Given the human rights crisis in East Asia, we need to act decisively. This is why I am deeply troubled that despite the egregious reports concerning North Korea and the national security threat it poses, the administration has still not appointed a U.S. Ambassador to South Korea.

It is critical that we have American diplomats on the ground. I also continue to be deeply troubled and critical of the administration and in particular President Trump's juvenile and unprofessional verbal attacks on the North Korean leadership.

Like the chair said, the regime—the cult has to be taken seriously and my concern is that these attacks, especially the nature of them—calling the North Korean leader names—these attacks diminish our ability to bring about change and, in my opinion, only reinforce the regime's propaganda that the U.S. is waiting to attack.

With that, Mr. Chair, I yield my time.

Mr. SMITH. Thank you very much, Ms. Bass.

I would like to now turn to Dan Donovan.

Mr. DONOVAN. Mr. Chairman, I'll yield my time so as to allow the witnesses more time to testify.

Thank you very much.

Mr. SMITH. Thank you very much, I'd say, to my friend.

Let me begin by welcoming our first panel. We have two panels today. Ms. Hyeona Ji, who is a North Korean defector, human rights activist, and writer. Her entire family decided to escape North Korea in 1998. Ms. Ji was soon arrested and repatriated to North Korea during the first repatriation in February 1998 and was harshly interrogated and beaten, and witnessed other repatriated North Koreans, including adults, children, pregnant women, undergo beatings and invasive searches for hidden money.

Ms. Ji escaped North Korea again in April 1998, leaving behind her younger brother, to search for her mother and sister in China.

She was caught by sex traffickers and sold for $25,000 Chinese yuan.

In April 1999, she was arrested by Chinese authorities again and forced to be repatriated again for the second time.

In November 2000, she escaped North Korea for the third time. In 2002 she was arrested and forcibly repatriated to North Korea again. This time, while 3 months pregnant upon her arrival in North Korea, she underwent a forced abortion without anesthetics, almost dying from blood loss at the hands of North Korean authorities.

Ms. Ji was about to be sentenced without a fair trial. But thanks to a compassionate security officer, she was able to avoid further incarceration and in October of that same year escaped North Korea again.

Since her arrival in South Korea in 2007, Ms. Ji has been very active as a human rights activist in South Korea and abroad, telling the world of her experience, of multiple escapes and forced repatriation. She is currently co-chairperson of the Worldwide Coalition to Stop Genocide in North Korea. We welcome her and are honored to have her testify today.

Our second witness will be Ms. Han Ga Hee, who was born in 1980 in North Korea. She studied at an ag college and worked as a laborer at a collective farm.

While in North Korea, she listened to the radio broadcast of Free North Korea Radio. The difficult conditions in North Korea and her curiosity led her to cross the border to go to China in 2002.

She worked various jobs in China but was always in constant danger of repatriation to North Korea. After 6 years in China, she saved up enough money to hire a broker to get her to South Korea.

After she paid him the money, the broker dropped her off at the border of Mongolia and handed her a compass and told her to head north across the grassland and the Gobi Desert.

Alone, she walked for several days without knowing where to go and finally was found by Mongolian police. Once she reached South Korea in '08, she went to visit the Free North Korea radio station and learned the truth.

All the people working there were defectors who fled North Korea. She has been working ever since for Free North Korea Radio—that's 8 years now—and has become a news announcer and is a producer of a gospel program.

We welcome her and are honored to have her testify as well.

STATEMENT OF MS. HYEONA JI, NORTH KOREAN DEFECTOR, CO-CHAIRPERSON, WORLDWIDE COALITION TO STOP GENOCIDE IN NORTH KOREA

[The following statement and answers were delivered through an interpreter.]

Ms. JI. Hello, my name is Hyeona Ji and I would like to express my appreciation to Members of Congress for your interest and concern for North Korean human rights.

In North Korea, the fact that 3 million people starved to death didn't seem out of the ordinary. The determination to escape from a country that denies its people freedom and human rights was stronger than the will to survive.

So I decided to leave North Korea, my close friends, neighbors, and my lovely hometown, and I left my fate up to the Tumen River at the border between China and North Korea.

In 1963, 3 years before the height of China's Cultural Revolution, my ethnic Korean-Chinese father, at the young age of 16, crossed the border into North Korea to find freedom.

In December 1997, he heard radio programs aired on the Korean Broadcasting System—KBS—while visiting family in China. Realizing that he had been duped his entire life, he came back to North Korea and persuaded the rest of us to leave North Korea.

So in February 1998, my father crossed the border in search of freedom again into China and by way of going upstream in the Tumen River, and with my mother and my two younger siblings we escaped via a lower part of the river downstream.

We were supposed to meet him at a predetermined location in China. But he was soon arrested—that's what we determined—and we have not known of his whereabouts for the last 19 years and my mother and two siblings and I were also immediately arrested and repatriated.

Afterward, I witnessed my mother being kicked with hard shoes for defecting and we were forced to sit down and stand up nearly 100 times doing the squatting motion in the process of being inspected for any illegal contraband, especially money, and we were subject to very severe thought criticism at the numerous agencies of the North Korean Government.

And, of course, our neighbors and friends gave us the cold shoulder. I was taken to and tortured at the Ministry of State Security for keeping a small Korean language Bible given to me from my mother, because in North Korea they don't allow freedom of religion.

I was released only after lying that I found it on the ground after severe beating and torture, and my mother and younger sister went to China and were supposed to return in a couple days. But they were kidnapped and sold.

And they went to China in search of food to bring back to the family but they were arrested and sold into this human trafficking situation. And my youngest sister, who was only 17 at the time, was sold and forced to marry an ethnic Chinese man who was over 40 years old.

I myself was also trafficked and so my brother lost all of us when he was only 10 years old when he was left back in North Korea. When I was repatriated a year later, that was when I began to witness the worst of North Korea's human rights atrocities.

At the Jeungsan Detention Facility, pregnant women were forced to do hard labor all day long. Because North Korea does not allow for mixed ethnicities, they made repatriated women who became pregnant in China to miscarry by forcing them to do hard labor.

At night we heard pregnant mothers screaming and babies dying without being able to see their mothers. I was reunited with my mother, whom I had not seen for a year, when I was sent to the provincial police jail because she herself was also repatriated, and because of the abuse and torture that I received at this facility, my bones and my rib were not healed properly and as a result I still suffer from that beating.

I was soon separated from my mother and then sent to the Jeungsan Re-education Camp Facility Number 11. This is the place where people that went in did not come out alive.

This is the place where people were forced to do hard labor and because of lack of food given to the inmates they were forced to eat locusts or skin live frogs and reptiles and rats and eat that to make up for the deficient food that was given to them, and many inmates died from malnutrition and from suffering from diarrhea.

Almost everyone who died was buried at a place that we inmates called Flower Hill. But everyone knew that the dead bodies ended up being food for the dogs belonging to the guard that kept watch over the burial site and these dogs belonged to the guard that was placed there to watch over the dead bodies.

At the Jeungsan Re-education Prison Camp Number 11, I was beaten with a wooden bar and kicked for not obeying commands on time and as a result of this beating and other mistreatment, not only did I suffer broken ribs that didn't heal properly, but to this day I suffer from chronic illnesses like epilepsy and fibromyalgia.

I was given a 1-year sentence but was pardoned after 8 months on Kim Jong-il's birthday on February 16th, 2000, and I escaped again, knowing that I had to tell the world about North Korea's human rights realities.

However, I was arrested and repatriated in China again for the third time and sent back to North Korea, this time 3 months pregnant, and I was forced to undergo an abortion without any medication at the police station in North Korea.

So my first child passed away without ever seeing the world and without any time for me to even say sorry to my child. Even though I was haemorrhaging to death, they were filling out papers to send me to the Hamheung Re-education Prison Camp without even a fair trial.

Thankfully, there was an officer on my case who took pity on me and let me be released from the prison due to my condition. Even though I was in terrible health, I crossed the Tumen River yet again to go into China.

I had to do this because I vowed to myself and I made a promise to the people that I saw at Jeungsan Prison Camp that I would survive and live the life that they never got to live.

And I made this vow crossing into China because I wanted to tell the world what the experience and to tell the people that I would survive and live the life that they, prisoners in Jeungsan, never got to live.

Between my first escape from North Korea in February 1998 and 2007, I was repatriated three times and escaped North Korea a total of four times.

I spent 8 months in a re-education center and some time in China, which was a foreign place to me, before finally reaching South Korea in 2007.

As soon as I arrived, I arranged for my mother and her daughter to come to Korea via Myanmar. But I had no news about my two younger siblings and father.

And then one day my brother arrived in South Korea and my brother had been on the street for—alone for 13 years and we could not do anything but hold him, embrace him and cry.

And the following year in 2011, my little sister, who was only 17 when I last saw her, made it to South Korea via Thailand at the age of 31. So we were reunited after 14 years of separation and we wept with joy and we vowed that we will never be separated again.

Right this moment, I miss my father terribly and this longing is not unique just for myself. It is a longing of all North Korean defectors. The recent case of the running of the defector soldier across the joint security area represents a dash toward freedom. That is the dream of 25 million North Korean people.

North Korea is one terrifying prison and the Kim regime is carrying out crimes against humanity in North Korea, and it is only a miracle that people and I, myself, survived the hellish experience of the prison camp.

However, the Chinese Government continues to send North Koreans seeking freedom back to this prison. On November 4th of this year, a mother and her child were detained on their way to meet their father in South Korea—in China.

The excitement of meeting his father was momentary because the Chinese Government sent them back on a deadly path back to North Korea.

China, which has lived through a so-called "Cultural Revolution," is well aware of what happens to repatriated defectors and how they will be treated. Yet, it continues to send North Koreans back.

How is this different from murder? I strongly urge the Chinese Government to discontinue and stop the forcible repatriation of North Korean refugees.

Much like the Apostle Paul, who says in the Gospel that he is indebted for the Gospel, I confess to my father and to those who have died in prison after repatriation and to all North Koreans that I am in debt for my freedom.

And so yesterday I asked the U.N. officials and today I ask Members of Congress and other people gathered throughout the world to fight for the freedom and human rights of North Koreans and repatriated defectors who do not even have the right to know or the right to own anything and who have no freedom at all in North Korea.

I will now read a poem that I wrote for a book of poetry that I wrote in memory of the prisoners that dies in the prison camp, and it is titled, "Is Anyone There?"

I am afraid. Is anyone out there?
This is hell. Is anyone out there?
Despite my urgent pleas, no one is opening the door for me.
Is anyone there?
Please hear our cries.
Hear the pain of us getting stepped on.
Is anyone there?
Is anyone there?
People are dying. My friend is dying also.
I am calling and calling. Why is there no answer?
Is there really no one there?

There's a poet—Dutch poet by the name of Job Degenaar and he said, "The doors to prison must be opened from the outside."

And so I appeal to you, to the United States, to South Korea, to all of us here to find many ways we can open the doors to North Korea.

And when you meet people from North Korea once it becomes a free country and the people of North Korea ask you, what have you done as earlier beneficiaries of freedom that we do not have, all of us will have a good answer in reply to those North Koreans.

Thank you.

[The prepared statement of Ms. Ji follows:]

Hyeona Ji
Representative, Worldwide Coalition to Stop Genocide in North Korea
Committee on Foreign Affairs, Subcommittee on Africa, Global Health, Global Human Rights, and
International Organizations.
"Protecting North Korean Refugees", Dec. 12th, 2017
Henry Song – Interpreter

In North Korea, the fact that 3 million people starved to death didn't seem out of the ordinary.

The determination to escape from a country that denies its people freedom and human rights was stronger than the will to survive. So I decided to leave North Korea, my close friends, neighbors, and lovely hometown and I left my fate up to the Tumen River at the border between China and North Korea. But I was separated from my father as soon as I set foot in China because of Chinese police rounding up North Korean defectors, and I was repatriated with my mother and two siblings.

It was 1963, three years before China's Cultural Revolution began, when my ethnic Korean-Chinese (*joseon-jok*) father, at the young age of 16, crossed the border into North Korea to find freedom. In December 1997, he heard radio programs aired on the Korean Broadcasting System while visiting family in China. Realizing he had been duped his entire life, he persuaded us to leave North Korea. So in February 1998, my father crossed the border in search of freedom again, this time, into China, by way of upstream Tumen River. My mother, two siblings, and I escaped via a route more downstream. We were supposed to meet him at a predetermined location in China, but we have not known of his whereabouts for the last 19 years. My mother, two siblings and I were immediately repatriated.

Afterward, I witnessed my mother kicked with hard shoes for defecting, and we were forced to sit down and stand up nearly 100 times in the process of being inspected for carrying money. We were subject to thought criticism at numerous agencies. Our neighbors and friends gave us the cold shoulder.

I was taken to and tortured at the Ministry of State Security for keeping a small Korean Bible given to me from my mother. You see, North Korea doesn't allow freedom of religion. I was released only after lying that I found it on the ground. My mother and younger sister went to China and were supposed to return in a couple of days, but they were kidnapped and sold. My little sister, at the young age of 17, was sold and forced to marry a man over 40.

I was also trafficked, so my brother lost all of us when he was just 10. When I was repatriated a year later, I witnessed the worst North Korea's human rights atrocities.

At the Cheongjin detention center, pregnant women were forced to hard labor all day. Because North Korea does not allow mixed ethnicities, they make women who have become pregnant in China to miscarry by forcing them to hard labor. At night, we heard pregnant mothers screaming, and babies died without being able to see their mothers. There was a woman who gave birth to a baby at night at 8 months after a full day of work. She was so happy to hold her child, but that moment was short lived. Soon after, a guard commanded her to drown her own newborn. She pleaded the guard for mercy with the baby in her arms, but in the end, she did as told. The image of the dead infant tore through my 20-year-old heart.

I was reunited with my mother, whom I had not seen for a year, when I was sent to the provincial police jail because she was also repatriated. But we were separated again, since I was sent to the Jeungsan Reeducation Center no. 11 without trial.

Not many made it out alive from this place. Everyone was subject to harsh labor, and meals were so lacking that we ate raw locusts, discarded cabbage leaves, and skinned frogs and rats. People died withered and dehydrated from continuous diarrhea.

I befriended a girl named Younghee. Her parents were shot dead and she was alone. We promised to survive this place and go to South Korea together. One day, we secretly ate some grass while working but got caught and were ordered to eat grass roots with dirt still on them. This caused Younghee diarrhea, and she eventually died from it. I could do nothing but weep and close her eyes after her death.

Almost everyone who dies there is buried at a place called "Flower Hill," but everyone knows that the dead bodies end up being food the dog belonging to the guard. My friend Younghee was no exception.

At Jeungsan Reeducation Center no. 11, I was beaten with a wooden bar and kicked for not obeying commands on time. I suffered a broken rib that healed at an angle, and I suffer chronic illnesses like epilepsy and fibromyalgia. I was given a 1-year sentence but was pardoned after 8 months on Kim Jong Il's birthday on Feb. 16, 2000. I embarked on my third escape knowing I had to tell the world about North Korea's human rights realities. But I was repatriated for the third time when I was three months pregnant and was forced an abortion without any medication at the local police station in North Korea.

So my first child passed away without ever seeing the world, without any time for me to apologize.

Even when I was hemorrhaging to death, they were filling out papers to send me to Hamheung Reeducation no. 55 without fair trial. Thankfully, the police officer on my case let me go on bail due to my condition.

Though I was in terrible health, I crossed the Tumen yet again.

I had to, because I vowed to myself as I closed the eyes of the dying at Jeungsan Reeducation Center no. 11, that I would survive to live the life they never got to live.

Between my first escape from North Korea in Feb. 1998 and 2007, I was repatriated 3 times and escaped a total of 4 times. I spent 8 months in a reeducation center and some time in China, a foreign place to me, before finally reaching South Korea in 2007.

As soon as I arrived, I arranged for my mother and my daughter to come to Korea via Myanmar, but I have no news about my two younger siblings and father.

Then one day, my brother arrived in South Korea. My brother had been on the streets alone for 13 years, and my mother could do nothing but cry while they embraced. And the next year, in 2011, my little sister who was 17 when I last saw her, made it to South Korea via Thailand at the age of 31. We hugged and wept endless tears at our first reunion in 14 years.

Right now, I miss my father terribly.

This longing is not unique. It is the longing of all North Korean defectors. The running of the recently defected North Korean soldier across the Joint Security Area represents a dash toward freedom that is the dream of 25 million North Koreans. North Korea is a terrifying prison, and it takes a miracle to survive there.

But the Chinese government sends North Koreans seeking freedom back to this prison.

On Nov. 4, a mother and her child were detained on the way to meet the father in South Korea. The excitement of meeting his dad was momentary, because the Chinese government sent them back on a deadly path.

China, which has lived through a so-called cultural revolution, is well aware of how repatriated defectors will be treated, yet it continues to send North Koreans back. How is this different from killing?

I strongly urge the Chinese government to discontinue forcible repatriation of North Koreans toward death. Much like Paul the Apostle, who says he is in debt for the Gospel, I confess, to my father, those who have died in prison after repatriation, and all North Koreans, that I am in debt for freedom.

I ask UN officials and representatives around the world, and members of the US Congress, to fight for the freedom and human rights of North Koreans and repatriated defectors, who do not even have the right to know or the right to own.

I want to share a poem I wrote, titled, "Is Anyone There?"

I am afraid, is anyone out there?
This is hell, is anyone out there?
Despite my urgent pleas, no one is opening the door for me.
Is anyone there?
Please, hear our cries.
Hear the pain of us getting stepped on. Is anyone there?
People are dying. My friend is dying also.
I am calling and calling, why is there no answer?
Is there really no one there?

The Dutch poet Job Degenaar said, "The doors to prison must be open from the outside." I appeal to you to find many ways we can open the doors to North Korea.

And when you mean people from the North once it becomes a free country, and they ask you "what have you done, as early beneficiaries of freedoms we did not have?" you have a good answer.

Thank you.

Mr. SMITH. Ms. Ji, thank you very much for that very moving and inspiring testimony and also your challenge to each of us to do more.

There are all of us out there but there needs to be more of us and we need to raise our voices even more effectively and louder as we go forward. So thank you for that call.

Ms. Hee.

STATEMENT OF MS. HAN GA HEE (ALIAS), NORTH KOREAN DEFECTOR, ANNOUNCER AND SOUND ENGINEER, FREE NORTH KOREA RADIO

[The following statement and answers were delivered through an interpreter.]

Ms. HEE. Hello. Thank you very much for this opportunity to be a witness in this hearing.

My name is Han Ga Hee. I escaped from North Korea into China and in China I was human trafficked, and while being trafficked I was given a Bible and the Bible became my light, and eventually I found my way to South Korea and I am here before you.

I am still living the fears that I had back in China. I had a knife put to my neck and the choice was either that I get married to a Chinese man living in the countryside or else. Those were the choices I had and those are the fears that I still live every night.

I was caught three times and I was sold three times, and after the third time that I was human trafficked I found an escape.

Since this was during winter time at minus 30 Celsius, I had escaped to ensure that my footprint would not be found. So I had to walk in the little stream that was there and as a result I had frostbite, and the frostbite keeps on reminding me of what happened. Every winter I get them back.

However, this is not something that I myself am the only one living with. It's something that many of the refugees from North Korea are living with and also especially true for children from North Korea.

What I had led was a very harsh life and what I had to endure was very dreadful. But for me, there was hope. The hope came in the name of freedom, Free North Korea Radio.

When I had initially heard the broadcasting on Free North Korea Radio, initially I had thought actually this was sort of a propagation by South Korea, possibly by the National Intelligence Service of the South Korean Government in order to lure North Koreans into South Korea.

There is a movie that's widely shown in North Korea. It's called "Psychological Warfare." Basically, the story goes South Korean Government lures North Korean people into South Korea, takes their intelligence, and kills them all.

When I watched the movie, I truly believed this was what was taking place, and not just me but I believe other North Koreans also believed that to be true.

Well, one of the programs that was quite impressive to me when I heard in China broadcasted by Free North Korea Radio was about Seong Hye-rim. The title of the program was, "I am Friend of Seong Hye-rim."

Seong Hye-rim is a wife to Kim Jong-il, and in that program I heard about all the women that Kim Jong-il and Kim Il-song around them and all the womanizing that took place. It was a shock to me because these are the very people that we had worshipped while we were in North Korea but I came to realize that they were trash of human beings.

And also, we had been told that Hwang Jang-yop, the Secretary, had been killed by commandoes sent by North Korea to South Korea. However, through the broadcasting we learned that he was alive and well and I heard his voice and many of the messages that he had sent for us.

While I was living in China, hiding from the authorities, I really wanted freedom and I realized freedom was not free—that I could not just sit still and try to get freedom. I had to find my way to freedom.

So what happened was in August 2008, I was given a compass and just a compass—that's all I had—and I walked across the deserts of Mongolia. I believe it was Gobi Desert that I crossed and eventually ended up in South Korea.

Even today, there are many North Koreans who are living in China and they want freedom. However, these people are in fear of the Chinese authorities who are repatriating these people to North Korea.

And when these North Koreans are repatriated back into North Korea, what is waiting for them is not all that pleasant. Many would be sent to political prisons. Others would be tortured and some may even be executed.

One time I was cut by the authorities and I was sent to a state security prison, and in the prison I stayed there for about 15 days. I recall there was a woman who was repatriated from China.

She was pregnant and the guards yelled out that she was pregnant with impure blood, and I believe that she was beaten to the point where the pregnancy was terminated.

However, the actual beating was not by the guards but at the command of the guards the North Korean men who were repatriated, these were the people who were forced into beating the woman, and what choice did these men have?

Well, it's laughable that on the World Human Rights Day that North Koreans would come out and say that they do respect human rights.

Well, these are the people who still, to this date, are carrying out public executions and also they consider their residents less than logs or coals.

Perhaps the biggest abuse of human rights by North Koreans would be starvation that North Korean people are having to suffer and also the nonprovision of the bare necessities that these people need to have as human beings.

And let me speak briefly on my father, who had to have his legs amputated. He went to China looking for food for us. However, he was caught and later had to amputate his legs for some reasons.

And why was it that he had to lose his legs? Well, after having been caught by the military, he was sent to a prison and at the prison actually he was facing the Tumen River on a certain night and he did not have anything on him.

He was completely naked and he was forced to kneel looking toward the Tumen River. It was minus 30 degrees Celsius and he was beaten by a leather belt and thereafter he was left kneeling, looking toward the river, for the night and as a result he had frostbite and his legs had to be amputated.

And after the amputation it didn't take long for his life to be ended. It is laughable that they would have a declaration of human rights when the regime itself is carrying out all these atrocities including stratification of people into classes based on who they were born or based on their lineages and not even providing the basic necessities required for human beings.

The ruthlessness of the North Korean regime has gotten even worse since Kim Jong-un has come into power in 2011. However, this tyranny cannot last forever. We know that.

And the very reason why he carries out these politics of fear is because there is collapse that's taking place internally in North Korea and this is very apparent by hearing from North Koreans who have escaped. One would be the very soldier who had escaped through the joint security area not too long ago and then there are other North Korean refugees who have been interviewed by our radio.

And what we do at the Free North Korea Radio is to listen to the refugees. We use their voices and we compare the lives of North Koreans and South Koreans and also tell the truth about what takes place outside of North Korea.

And what we do is we have network of people in North Korea including elites of North Korea who would be provide intelligence and information to us and those information are disseminated through broadcasting.

Included in our activities are not just the broadcasting but also sending materials into North Korea by way of crossing the border between China and North Korea.

We have sent many USBs, SD cards, CD players, and radios to North Korea, and of the refugees that have been surveyed, 5 to 10 percent of the people have stated that they have actually heard broadcasting through Free North Korea Radio.

When we are talking about North Korea, they are completely eliminating flow of information from outside. When you say 5 to 10 percent of people have heard, that's a lot of numbers.

And also for 10 minutes per day we have music that's played. But this is actually a play on words because we use the North Korean music but we change the lyrics so that it's not about Kim Jong-un or Kim Jong-il any longer.

For example, there would be music titled, "In My Father's Footsteps" and we would switch the word father into Jesus, and also that "We trust in the general" the general would be changed into "in our God."

By using the tunes that are familiar to North Koreans but changing the lyrics, it's gotten easier for us to get the information into North Korea and into the heads of these people.

My mother still remains in North Korea and I have heard through certain people that she's doing okay and that she's also worshiping the God that I believe in.

So the sarcastic saying is that amongst North Korean people North Korea is known as a capitalistic society with a twist, and what that tells us is that there is tremendous internal collapse that's taking place in North Korea.

And that is why Kim Jong-un is ruling by fear. He knows that his control and grasp on North Korean people is slipping.

Mr. SMITH. If I could just interrupt 1 second, and I would ask you to continue your testimony momentarily.

Just to ask a couple of questions—I have to leave. One of my bills, H.R. 3655, is on the floor in about 5 or 10 minutes. I will come back as soon as it's over.

Dan Donovan, thankfully, has agreed to take the chair. So please come back. But I would want you and Ms. Ji to address, if you would, you have said that Kim Jong-un—it's even worse.

Suzanne Scholte, who is the sole Peace Prize Laureate who has testified numerous times before this and other committees of Congress, points out that it's even worse under Xi Jinping because of his policies.

So it's worse in China. It's worse in North Korea under Kim Jong-un. If you could elaborate on that it would be very helpful.

If we were a panel of Chinese leaders, what would you say to them, especially it is illegal for them to forcibly repatriate North Korean defectors pursuant to the Refugee Convention to which, as we all know, they are signatories to.

And finally, if you could speak to the issue of the cult of Kim— the godlike cult that they—and Juche that they inculcate beginning from the earliest years. How did you break out from that, since the propaganda is ever present and all—other than the great work you're doing, the information flow almost never happens during all of those formative years. So people come to believe that Kim is God—if you could speak to that.

And I will have to read your answers on the transcript as I run off to this hearing.

VOICE. Can she finish her prepared statement?

Mr. SMITH. Of course. Please finish it. Exactly.

Ms. HEE. And in times like this, it's more important that we get the right information into North Korea so we need to make sure that there is a steady flow of information into North Korea so the people in North Korea would come to realize what is really taking place out there.

And so my focus is really on information flow. We need to have more information, more truth be told to the people of North Korea, to have this information flowing into North Korea, and in this regard we seek help from the U.S. Government and the U.S. Congress.

And I hope and I believe, once we have this information going into North Korea that the collapse of North Korea would be not in the distant future but tomorrow.

Thank you.

[The prepared statement of Ms. Hee follows:]

Ms. Han Ga Hee
North Korean Defector
Announcer and Sound Engineer, Free North Korea Radio
House Committee on Foreign Affairs
Subcommittee on Africa, Global Health, Global Human Rights, and International Organizations
"Protecting North Korean Refugees"   **Tuesday, December 12, 2017**

Good afternoon, everyone.

Thank you so much for having me in this hearing to testify in front of honorable members of the Congress.

My name is Han Ga-hee. I am a defector who met with God in China and could defect to South Korea because of His Grace.

I was a victim of human trafficking. Throughout all those dark days of my life in China, the only light I saw was from the Bible which someone I met in China handed to me.

When the traffickers sold me to a Chinese man, and threatened me with a knife as I resisted, I still could have hope and survive to get to the land of freedom, and I believe it was because I would not worship and pledge my allegiance to the Kim Regime in North Korea and sought my freedom in God.

What I found in South Korea was truly shocking and overwhelming to me; the United States is not the evil invader who threatens North Korea, but on contrary, they are in the front line to fight for the freedom and human rights of North Koreans, my parents, brothers and sisters, and myself, who are living under the lies of the dictatorship.

This is what I would have never known if I did not listen to Free North Korea Radio when I was in China.

I was an avid fan of Chinese and South Korean soap-operas even before I left North Korea in 2002, and also often listened to the radio broadcasting to North Korea, which was run by South Korean government back then. But it was not until few years later that I heard the familiar voices of North Korean defectors through the transistor radio. One day, through my defector friend at church, I heard about Free North Korea Radio, the independent radio station broadcasting to North Korea, just started their service, and while listening to their programs, I learned the term 'North Korean defector' for the first time.

At first I thought it was a scheme of South Korean National Intelligence Service to lure North Koreans to get them to South Korea for propaganda purpose.

The reason why I thought like that was because it was exactly the same plot of a propaganda movie called 'Operation Psychology'. The movie is about how the South Korean government lures North Koreans, takes all their important information and kills them. Without any doubt, I truly believed that the movie was a real story. Not only myself, but any North Korean who saw the movie would have the same thought.

However, as I listened to the programs of Free North Korea Radio every day, listening to my fellow North Koreans speaking from Seoul to their friends and family in North Korea, my suspicion melted away and I finally decided to defect to South Korea.

The most impressive piece I have ever heard from Free North Korea Radio was the program called 'I was the friend of Seong Hye-rim', talking about Kim Il-sung and Kim Jong-il's affairs with many women. It divulged how corrupt and immoral, 'human trash' they were, which startled me who had naively worshiped and admired them as Great Father. The most shocking thing was hearing Hwang Jang-yop, the creator of the Juche Ideology, and of whom North Korean regime said in their propaganda had been assassinated by the South Korean government.   But, he was alive and well and on the Free North Korea Radio's program and giving a speech. It was truly an eye-opening experience to learn about the world, and how blind I had been.

Then, I had to decide hiding in dreadful fear of repatriation.   My life was at the crossroads to death and life. I could stay in China, or I could fight for life and freedom which was not free. I believed that seeking freedom, although it could put my life in danger, was better than just hiding in China and waiting for death. So in August 2008, I left China to go to South Korea.

Throughout my journey, I was with my old Bible all the time. For me, it was hard to even understand what the words meant, but I read it through twice. And I prayed and prayed God to lead my way safe, and let me get to South Korea as soon as possible so that I could speak to my fellow North Koreans living under the darkness with my own voice and deliver the message of truth. I crossed the Gobi Desert to get to Mongolia. All I had in my hands were a compass that the broker gave me and told me to just head North. When there seemed to be no road, God's love and grace led my way, and after eight months, I finally arrived in South Korea.

The first thing I did after the arrival was to find whether Free North Korea Radio really existed. As I finished the resettlement training program, I visited the station. To my greatest surprise, it was actually run solely by North Korean defectors.

Finding all the things I had known about the station were true, I decided to devote myself to its work to speak to my friends and family in North Korea. Back then, I had never even known what a computer was, but I determined to self-train to become a sound engineer, and since 2010 I have been working at Free North Korea Radio as a sound engineer as well as an announcer.

I know my work can put my family still living in North Korea at risk, but someone has to carry on this operation, and if I shun my work, the day which North Korea can rejoice with freedom and light might never come.

'Freedom is not free.' This sentence which I saw at the Korean War Memorial here in Washington, D.C. is now the compass in my heart pointing the road to life, and makes me grateful for everything I am enjoying right now.

There are so many things that I want to tell you today, but I understand there's a time limit. So I will stop here. Thank you so much for listening to my story.

*Here below is the testimonies of North Korean defectors who decided to defect after listening to Free North Korea Radio, just like me.

First of all, the strongest advantage of Free North Korea Radio over other radio stations comes from the fact that it is run by North Korean defectors; they know the North Koreans as well as the society the most and the best. The information they deliver to North Koreans comes from their own experiences living in both South and North Korean society. This is why their words explaining the truth about North Korean dictatorship is well received by the listeners.

Since its first operation in 2004, Free North Korea Radio has the widest network of stringers in a variety of levels of North Korean society, covering from top level elites in the Central Party and government to ordinary citizens in the border areas.

From such a network, Free North Korea Radio has covered several exclusives about North Korea, including the execution of Jang Sung-Thaek, the uncle of Kim Jong-un, and the currency reform in 2009.

Also, according to the surveys of 100 to 200 recent defectors which Free North Korea Radio conducts two times a year, 5 to 10 percent of respondents answer that they decided to defect after listening to Free North Korea Radio; some of them even give the specific titles of the programs that influenced them, such as 'South Korea, in the Eye of North Korean defectors', 'A Diary of North Korean Defector Student' and 'The Last Woman of Kim Jong-il.'

The respondents often say that the radio programs produced by South Korean broadcasting stations feel somewhat distant because of their South Korean accents, but the message Free North Korea Radio delivers is more easily received as it feels like one of their friends is talking to them. Also, after they listened to Free North Korea Radio's program on capitalism and market economy, young North Koreans started to compare the economic system they had, and even derided that North Korea is a country with a very unique capitalist system.

Among our listeners, there are people who got to know God as they listened to the mission programs which airs 15 minutes every day. Also, like myself, there are North Korean refugees in China who call to the station to ask for help to come to South Korea. Free North Korea Radio has been actively engaged in rescues of these North Korean refugees.

Lastly, I also attach the pictures on Free North Korea Radio's operation in the last year. I hope this information would give the idea to US Congress about how actively the station has been working to create greater information inflow to North Korea.

I sincerely hope that the US government and US Congress can help North Korean defector organizations, who are at the frontier of sending in information to North Korea, and who are working vigorously in order to bring freedom to North Koreans and end the oppression they live under because of the Kim dictatorship.

Thank you very much.

———

Mr. DONOVAN [presiding]. Thank you, Ms. Hee.

I am not too sure if you remember the chairman's questions. He wanted those answered. So he could read the transcript.

So I'd ask Ms. Ji if you would answer the chairman's questions first and then, Ms. Hee, you can answer the questions as well.

Ms. JI. So I'll answer the congressman's second part of the question, which was if Chinese leaders were sitting in front of me how I would address them, and the first thing I would tell them is that the Chinese Government must stop the policy of forced repatriation of North Korean defectors back to North Korea.

And North Korean defector women have become sort of a commodity in the sense that when they are being led away by unscrupulous Chinese brokers, the Chinese security apparatus members, some of them they will intercept this transaction and they themselves will get involved with the human trafficking and, in turn, sell the women to the highest bidder to other brokers. So this is happening in China right now among the security people of China.

And I myself explain exactly that. I was actually in the process of being sold by the Chinese security officials. But because I was screaming and resisting so much, that's how I was able to escape when they were sort of stunned at my resistance that I showed to them when I was undergoing this treatment.

North Korean defector women are not commodity. They are not material goods. They are human beings. And the fact that the Chinese Government officials—security officials—are—some of them are being involved with this is something that the international community should not forget or forgive.

And the second thing that I would tell the Chinese officials if they were sitting in front of me in this room would be that the North Korean defector women who are forced to marry the Chinese men, the mothers themselves are basically stateless.

But when they become pregnant by the so-called Chinese husband, the children that they bear they are stateless too. They have no identity. They don't exist, according to the Chinese Government. And in China right now, the mothers of these children, many of them have been repatriated back to North Korea.

So you have a lot of kids who are either orphans or who do not have mothers or they basically are not cared for. So a lot of these children born to Chinese fathers and North Korean defector women are living in a very difficult situation in China right now.

And what I would desire is that either process these children to be sent to South Korea or grant them some sort of identification or citizenship in China to these children born to Chinese husbands and North Korean defector mothers.

And lastly, I would urge the Chinese Government to keep its promise as a signatory to the convention relating to status of refugees and to faithfully carry out its duties as a signatory to that convention by protecting the North Korean defectors that come into China instead of repatriating them.

Lastly, I would say, as I mentioned in my testimony, North Korean defectors, when they are repatriated from China to North Korea, they face unspeakable inhumane treatment, sometimes even death, at the hands of the North Korean authorities.

So the Chinese Government should accept the North Korean defectors that come to China and process them to be sent to South Korea.

Mr. DONOVAN. Thank you very much.

Ms. Hee, would you mind answering the chairman's questions?

Ms. HEE. You ask how the current Kim Jong-un regime is different from the previous Kim Jong-il regime.

Well, he is ruling by fear and it's very much of a fear that's being put into the minds of North Koreans. Kim Jong-un is a child who does not know the season and who in their right mind would want to go up against a superpower that is the U.S. and threaten the U.S. with nuclear capabilities that are not even completely mature?

Well, my mom tells me when Kim Jong-il was in power, when celebratory occasions, on holidays, that there would be rationing provided by the government. But now that Kim Jong-un is in power, we don't have any rationing at all on any occasion.

And the rule of fear or rule by fear is one strike, you're out. There are no generosities to be exhibited. We are not aware of any government upon change of power to have over 300 elites of the government be publicly executed by way of air guns. Actually, that would be anti-aircraft artillery. And why? Why does he do that? Because he wants to rule by fear and this is the way he does it.

And Kim Jong-un will continue to rule by fear. The way we will be able to stop the rule by fear is not by restraining him but alerting and raising the awareness amongst North Korean people as to what's taking place outside, epically true about South Korea—how much of a freedom and economic prosperity that we live in.

And tying into the question about China, well, in order for us to be able to stop this ruling by fear, the pressure should not be on North Korea alone. The pressure should also be on China.

What is true before is also true now, that China and the Chinese people would say that they are pressuring North Korea. No pressure there.

Do you know why Chinese authorities repatriate North Koreans back to North Korea? For each person that's repatriated there is a return. They get logs and they get coal.

The way I was caught by the Chinese authorities was an informant talked about me and I understand that that informant was getting 2,000 Chinese yuan. So per report that they make, they get 2,000 yuan.

So when I was caught by the Chinese authorities, who are known as Gong An, I asked them why do you have to take me and why do you need to send me back to North Korea and what one of the officers had told me was that he had to make a living and this was an agreement between the governments.

They know very well that once we are repatriated we will be suffering at the hands of North Korean guards. So the basic idea—there is a math—that we may die once we get back to North Korea but Chinese people would be getting the logs and coal.

So about 70 percent of the North Korean territory and the seas are really actually mined by the Chinese people. So when that is true, would Chinese people really want to put the pressure on North Korea and would they really want unification on the Peninsula?

So we can talk all day and we can have all these slogans asking for Chinese to put more pressure on North Korea. But these would be empty slogans. Nothing would come of them. We need to have real pressure that can be felt by the Chinese people.

Thank you.

Mr. DONOVAN. Thank you very much. Thank you, both of you, for your opening statements. Thank you for sharing your horrific experiences with us.

I'd just like to ask one or two questions and then we have a second panel, and you've been sitting there graciously for over an hour for us.

About 70 percent of the people, refugees from North Korea, are women. Why is that? Why do you feel most of the refugees are women?

Ms. HEE. It's a strange question to answer but it's a good question nevertheless, because we don't know why. But in North Korea we have more women than men.

And also men are serving in the military. It's mandatory. They have to serve for 13 years. So when you are stuck in a system for 13 years you're not getting out easy.

For a woman, once we escape to China we have other means for making a living. We can work in restaurants and we may even be trafficked. But still, we get to eat. But that does not happen for men. There are not a lot of things that they can do in China and also once they go to China they get captured a lot easier. It's just simply very hard for men to hide in China.

Mr. DONOVAN. Thank you very much.

I would just ask you, you were talking about when women refugees then marry a Chinese man and have a baby, is the baby repatriated back with the mother back to North Korea once you're captured and if so, is there a difference if the child is a boy compared to if the child is a girl?

Ms. JI. I myself personally did not witness the children born to defector women and Chinese fathers being repatriated together with the North Korean defector women.

However, I am aware that there are cases where the children born to—even though I haven't seen it myself, I am aware that that does happen where the children born to the defector women and the Chinese fathers are—if they are arrested together are sent back—repatriated back to North Korea.

And regardless of whether that child is a boy or girl, there is no difference in the eyes of the North Korean regime, and usually they are sent to an orphanage and the mothers are sent to a re-education prison camp for punishment.

Mr. DONOVAN. I was curious if the Chinese saw a difference between a boy being born to a Chinese man.

Ms. JI. The Chinese family members of the husband, if the mother—the defector woman—gives birth to a boy, they prefer sons, obviously. So they would prevent the mother from getting pregnant again because if they have a boy then they are satisfied.

That's what they would want, to just keep it at that in terms of the viewpoint of the Chinese family and the Chinese husband.

Mr. DONOVAN. Before I yield to Mr. Castro, if I could just ask each of you—I think you touched on it in your opening statement,

Ms. Hee—but what would you like to see the United States Government do?

Ms. JI. Well, first of all, I would like to thank the U.S. Government for its great interest and concern for the North Korean human rights issue and also for, in recent days, pressing for the increase and stronger sanctions to punish the North Korean regime.

So I would like to express, first of all, my appreciation for that position taken by the U.S. Government in terms of dealing with the North Korean regime.

But I believe a stronger sanctions enforcement should be put in place by the U.S. Government toward the North Korean regime.

And in addition to strengthening sanctions against the regime, the U.S. Government should expand and increase the activities of information dissemination into North Korea, and the latest ways that the U.S. can do that is to provide internet by using satellite, for example, and that's one way that the U.S. Government can help bring outside information to the North Korean people directly, bypassing the regime's control.

Mr. DONOVAN. Ms. Hee.

Ms. HEE. Would it be okay if I were to address an earlier question about repatriation of kids?

Mr. DONOVAN. Yes. Certainly.

Ms. HEE. Yes, that does take place in China. So under two separate scenarios, one would be if, as a mother, you are caught on the streets with your child, then you would both get repatriated. And also, if there is a raid and the child does not want to detach itself from the mother, then they both get repatriated.

And who actually does the repatriation? The Chinese Government. That's what they do. They are smiling behind their curtains, and we have all these slogans—all these empty slogans that are not heard by anybody in China.

Mr. DONOVAN. My last question the committee would like to have at least on the record about reports recently that the Chinese Government is building at least five refugee camps along the border. I am curious whether your sources can confirm that and what you think that may mean.

Ms. HEE. I believe that's in the news but I don't believe that was confirmed yet and through our sources we have not been able to confirm it. So maybe it's not happening.

Ms. JI. So I myself, even though I've heard of those reports of the Chinese Government supposedly building these facilities, I don't know for sure but I do know for a fact that through people that have contacted me from inside China and other sources that the Chinese Government, they fear a rush of North Korean people escaping from North Korea in case there is a war or some sort of major event happening.

So to prevent that that the Chinese Government on the Chinese side of the border they have reinforced the surveillance and the security in the region, for example, putting up more electrified fences and strengthening on the Chinese side their mechanisms to prevent North Koreans from crossing over in case of a major event.

Mr. DONOVAN. I thank you both for your diligence and the chair now recognizes the gentleman from Texas, Mr. Castro.

Mr. CASTRO. Thank you. Thank you for your courage and your bravery and also for coming here to testify today.

I have a question about the families that are left behind after people leave North Korea, after they defect. How are those family members treated after people leave North Korea?

Ms. HEE. I escaped alone. I have my family still in North Korea. I think my family is still safe. That's because North Korean authorities do not really know that I am here.

So I have also feared for the safety of my family and so I have thus far not worked in the open. So in November of this year, I had a teleconversation with my mom and I told mom that I would like to do more activities in the open regarding human rights, and this would bring about unification on the Korean Peninsula sooner, I told her.

But I also told her I was very much in fear for her welfare. And what my mom told me was that each day it's becoming harder for her to breathe and that she would die one way or another.

She didn't care, and she told me that I should do what I thought was the right thing to do. And that is why I am now in the open for 8 years working for Free North Korea Radio. No one knew of my identity. Now, perhaps, they do.

Mr. CASTRO. And you live in South Korea now?

Ms. HEE. Yes.

Mr. CASTRO. Okay. I have a follow-up question but I wanted to give you an opportunity to answer the same question.

Ms. JI. So as I mentioned in my testimony, all my family members are with me in South Korea except for my father, who has been missing for the past 19 years, and I have been able to get in touch with my aunt, who is still in North Korea. I have been able to send her money and also every once in a while call her as well.

But it's been about 10 years since I've been an active human rights activist out in the open. I've written two books already.

But it's been more than a year that I have had trouble trying to get in touch with my aunt. So perhaps the regime has finally caught up to what I am doing and perhaps did something to my aunt. I don't know. But it's been hard for me to get in touch with my aunt.

Mr. CASTRO. You don't know if she's been punished or what happened?

Ms. JI. So I was able to send somebody through, using brokers and through sending money to send somebody to my aunt's house in her village. But the report I got back was that the house was empty. There was nobody at the house. So something happened to my aunt. I just don't know exactly what happened to her.

Mr. CASTRO. And are you living in Seoul now or in South Korea?

Ms. JI. Yes, I am living in South Korea.

Mr. CASTRO. Well, I have a question for both of you.

One of the goals for a long time for the people of South Korea and, I imagine, many people in North Korea has been for unification of what for decades now has been two separate countries.

And I asked the same question of another defector when we did a larger Foreign Affairs panel—the main committee panel—a few months ago.

Is reunification realistic, given the fact that these countries have been separate countries now for many decades and you have now seen both societies—both North Korea and South Korea.

How significant are the differences? Can those differences be bridged for reunification?

Ms. JI. So as you mentioned, I did experience both life in North Korea and now I am living in South Korea, and North Korea is a Communist regime and South Korea is a free market capitalist society.

And for me, upon my first time being in South Korea as I started my resettlement it was very difficult for me to adjust to a life of freedom and a free market capitalist environment.

However, after some time I was able to adjust very well into this democratic free society in South Korea and so far there have been up to around 32,000 North Korean defectors that have resettled in South Korea and out of the 32,000 defectors I would say about 80 percent of those defectors in South Korea like myself are able to send money to our relatives and family members in North Korea.

So I have heard from not only the sources in North Korea but from other sources as well that many North Korean people in North Korea who have family members in South Korea have been aware that South Korea is a country that is rich, that is abundant, and that South Korean products are sought after, and that in some cases the high-ranking officials even want to marry off their children to family members of North Koreans who have people that have escaped to South Korea because that means they are able to get money from their relatives in South Korea.

So that's been the sort of shift that's happened in North Korea regarding their views on South Korea and South Koreans.

And you mentioned the differences between North Korea and South Korea. So I would say that even though North Korea may be a Communist system on the outside, but inside the people, because of the emerging markets and because of the capitalist ventures started by many citizens in North Korea, many North Korean citizens are more aware of and they have become very well attuned to the free market capitalist ideals that we would find in South Korea, for example.

And I personally believe that this may lead to a quicker fall of the regime and an even faster reunification of the two Koreas in the Korean Peninsula.

Mr. CASTRO. I yield back. Thank you.

Mr. SMITH [presiding]. Thank you.

I want to thank our very distinguished and courageous panel for your testimony and, above all, for your life's work, which has been extraordinary.

And some day, when North Koreans are free you will be among the true heroes who helped make it happen. So thank you so very much.

Ms. JI. Thank you very much.

Mr. SMITH. Dan, thank you.

I would like to now welcome our second panel, if I could, to the witness table, beginning first with Ambassador Robert King, and I want to say a big welcome back to Dr. King, who, for so many years, sat over here with Tom Lantos as his top chief of staff. So it's great to have Ambassador King back.

He, as I think most will know, was our special envoy for North Korean human rights issues from 2009 to 2017. Since leaving the department he is senior advisor to the Korea chair at the Center for Strategic and International Studies.

For 25 years—a quarter of a century—from '83 to '08 Ambassador King served as chief of staff to Congressman Tom Lantos when Mr. Lantos became ranking minority member and then chair of the House Foreign Affairs Committee.

Dr. King served as committee staff director, and that was from '01 to 2008. In addition to his full time jobs, Dr. King has taught courses in U.S. foreign policy and international relations at the University of Southern California German study program, Brigham Young University study abroad program, American University in Washington, DC, New England College in New Hampshire.

Ambassador King is the author of five books and over 40 articles on international relations topics. We welcome him back again to the committee.

I would like to then welcome and introduce Greg Scarlatoiu with the Committee for Human Rights in North Korea. He's the executive director of the committee.

He has coordinated 20 HRNK publications addressing North Korea's human rights situation and the operation of its regime. He is a visiting professor at the Hankuk University of Foreign Studies in Seoul as well as instructor and coordinator of the Korean Peninsula and Japan class at the U.S. Department of State's Foreign Service Institute.

Prior to HRNK, Mr. Scarlatoiu was with the Korea Economic Institute. He has over 6 years of experience in international development on projects by the U.S. Agency for International Development, the World Bank, and the Asia Development Bank.

In 14 years he has authored and broadcast weekly in the Korean language. It's called the Scarlatoiu Column and it's with Radio Free Asia.

A seasoned lecturer on Korean issues, Mr. Scarlatoiu is a frequent commentator for CNN, BBC, Al Jazeera, Voice of America, Radio Free Asia, and other media operations. He has appeared as an expert witness at several congressional hearings on North Korean human rights and so we welcome him back today as well.

And our third distinguished panelist will be Suzanne Scholte, who is also making a trip back and in the past has provided expert witnesses to this subcommittee and other committees of Congress including, as I mentioned earlier, the first women who were ever trafficked that came forward and spoke at a congressional hearing—trafficked, that is, from North Korea into China—and it was extraordinarily moving testimony.

She is considered one of the world's leading activists in the North Korean human rights movement. She has spent the past two decades promoting the freedom and dignity of the North Korean people and is currently president of the Defense Forum Foundation, a nonprofit foundation promoting a strong national defense and freedom, democracy, and human rights abroad.

In 1996, she began a program to host the first North Korean defectors in the United States, giving them a voice to speak out about atrocities being committed against the people of North Korea including the political prison camps and the horrific treatment of refugees.

She has led international efforts to pressure China to end their horrific repatriation policy and has been involved in the rescue of hundreds of North Koreans escaping their country.

Currently, she also serves as the chairwoman of the North Korea Freedom Coalition, vice co-chair of the Committee for Human Rights in North Korea, and honorary chair of the Free North Korea Radio.

I welcome all three of our distinguished panelists and I yield the floor to Dr. King.

STATEMENT OF THE HONORABLE ROBERT KING, SENIOR ADVISER, KOREA CHAIR, CENTER FOR STRATEGIC AND INTERNATIONAL STUDIES (FORMER U.S. SPECIAL ENVOY FOR NORTH KOREAN HUMAN RIGHTS ISSUES)

Mr. KING. Thank you very much, Mr. Chairman.

It's a pleasure to be back with you again. Usually I sat on the other side behind you and Mr. Lantos. It's a different position to be down here today but I am glad to be "home."

I want to thank you for your focus on human rights and for what you have done with the subcommittee in terms of calling attention to these issues and problems.

I want to commend you on the caliber of the witnesses—the other witnesses that have testified today. It was extremely helpful to have these two women who have, at great difficulty, been able to leave North Korea and talk about their experiences, and again, it's a pleasure to be here with Greg and with Suzanne to talk about these issues.

Refugees or defectors who have chosen to leave North Korea is one of the key issues in the broader question of human rights in the North.

There has been a steady flow of defectors from the North since the famine of the late 1990s. Over the last two decades, some 30,000 North Koreans have fled the country. The vast majority have resettled in South Korea.

The concern of Americans to help these defectors from the North was one of the principal factors behind the adoption of the North Korea Human Rights Act in 2004.

Since the adoption of that legislation, the State Department and other Federal agencies have helped some 250 North Korean refugees resettle in the United States.

Most refugees, however, have chosen to settle in South Korea because of the familiarity of language and culture, as well as to join family members who are already there.

The number of refugees leaving North Korea annually has recently declined. The high point, in about 2011, was some 3,000 annually.

But tighter control of the borders by the North and difficulty getting through China has caused that number to fall to less than

1,500 last year. The numbers this year look like they will be even lower.

Virtually all defectors who flee North Korea today do so through China. Very, very few have been able to cross the inner-Korean border.

A few weeks ago we saw a very rare exception when a North Korean soldier was seriously wounded as he tried to escape and fled through the DMZ.

This indicates both the danger and how uncommon it is for defectors to go directly from the North into South Korea.

For those who escape through China, there are very serious problems from being trafficked, sold as virtual slaves, or being returned to the North.

In the past, when relations were good between China and North Korea, most defectors captured in China were quickly returned to North Korea where they were sent to brutal re-education camps that earlier witnesses have talked about here.

A couple of years ago, I had a particularly memorable conversation in South Korea with a young women who had fled the North. She was finally able to reach the South.

I asked her if this had been her first attempt. She said, "Oh, no. This was my sixth try." Five times previously, she sought to leave. Five times she was captured either in North Korea before she left or as she crossed into China.

She was returned to North Korean authorities and spent many months each time in a re-education camp where she was brutally treated.

On her sixth attempt, she and a friend who was going to leave with her, decided to go but they also decided to take with them poison tablets. Rather than be forcibly returned again and sent to a re-education camp they would have taken their own lives.

In the past, Mr. Chairman, when Chinese relations with South Korea have been good and China's relationship with the North has been strained, defectors have been allowed to go to South Korea.

A couple of years ago in a very highly unusual arrangement, China allowed some 13 or 14 North Korean restaurant workers to fly directly from China to South Korea where they were resettled.

A year or so ago, however, after the United States, with the cooperation and approval of the South Korean Government, established a THAAD missile battery in the South, this led to strained relations between China and South Korea.

Since that time, it has, again, been more difficult for defectors from the North to reach South Korea through China.

The United States Government has strongly supported South Korean efforts to assist defectors reach the South. On many occasions, I personally raised with senior Chinese Government officials our concern that defectors be permitted to flee the North, if that was their wish.

I know that other, more senior State Department officials have also raised this matter with senior Chinese officials.

Mr. Chairman, it's important that the United States continue to urge China to allow defectors to resettle elsewhere and if they wish to go to the South, our Government should continue to support South Korean Government efforts to help those people.

Congressional support for refugees such as through the reauthorization of the North Korea Human Rights Act is important, and I urge approval of that reauthorization legislation. It has already been adopted in the House. It's now awaiting action in the Senate. But it's urgent and it's important that the legislation be reauthorized.

A second matter that I was asked to talk about was the issue of providing free and unfettered information to the people of North Korea. The availability of accurate information about events beyond the borders in the North is extremely important to the North Korean people.

Information limits Pyongyang's ability to manipulate its own citizens, and we must continue to encourage the free flow of information into North Korea. Although it is illegal to own a radio or television capable of being tuned to stations other than the official government station, based on survey research we estimate that as many as a third of North Koreans listen to foreign radio broadcasts, particularly programs from Voice of America and Radio Free Asia funded by U.S. congressional appropriations.

These are extremely important. There are other creative and innovative programs which we fund—the U.S. Government funds—to get digital information to the North Korean people. These efforts need to be fully funded, encouraged, and expanded.

Mr. Chairman, military options against North Korea are severely limited. But one thing that we can do that will encourage positive change in the North is to increase the flow of accurate information from the outside world.

Our human rights efforts are an important aspect of our policy toward North Korea. We must not underestimate the value and importance of those efforts.

Thank you very much, Mr. Chairman. I look forward to any questions that you have.

[The prepared statement of Mr. King follows:]

Testimony of

Ambassador Robert R. King

*Senior Advisor to the Korea Chair, Center for Strategic and International Studies
and former U.S. Special Envoy for North Korea Human Rights Issues*

Hearing on "Protecting North Korean Refugees"
*Subcommittee on Africa, Global Health, and Human Rights
House Foreign Affairs Committee*

December 12, 2017

Chairman Smith, Ranking Member Bass, Members of the Committee—

It is a great pleasure for me to testify before this Subcommittee. It is almost nine years since I left the House Foreign Affairs Committee staff to join the Department of State. During the 25 years that I was chief of staff to Congressman Tom Lantos, a good portion of that time was also spent as a member of the Foreign Affairs Committee staff. It is nice to come "home."

I want to thank you for your focus on human rights issues. I respect your commitment to human rights around the world. When I was chief of staff to Congressman Lantos, he was Ranking Member during a part of the time you were Chair of the Human Rights Subcommittee. I remember some of the marathon hearings you held on human rights issues.

Mr. Chairman, I want to commend you on the caliber of the other witnesses you have invited to testify today. It was extremely helpful to hear from these defectors who left North Korea and found refuge elsewhere. Also on this panel, Greg Scarlatoiu, the Executive Director of the Committee for Human Rights in North Korea, has produced a series of extremely important studies on human rights abuses in the North. Suzanne Scholte has been an energetic voice for aiding North Korean defectors and mobilizing opinion against the abuses of the DPRK. It is an honor for me to appear with them.

The issue of refugees or "defectors" who have chosen to leave North Korea is the principal topic of the hearing today. It is also a key issue in dealing with the broader issue of human rights in the North. There has been a steady flow of defectors from the North since the famine in the late 1990s. Initially the refugees were desperate, starving people looking for work opportunities in China. Many of them subsequently went on to South Korea. Over the last two decades some 30,000 North Koreans have fled the North and have resettled in South Korea.

The interest of Americans in helping defectors from the North and the Congressional focus on this issue was the principal factor behind the adoption of the North Korea Human Rights Act in 2004 and its subsequent reauthorization. Provisions of that legislation called for Federal assistance to defectors who sought to flee to America. Since that legislation was adopted, the State Department and other Federal agencies have helped some 250 North Korean refugees resettle in the United States. Most refugees, however, have chosen to settle in South Korea because of the familiar language and culture, as well as family members already living there.

The number of refugees leaving the North annually has recently declined. The high point of nearly 3,000 was reached in 2011, but tighter control of the borders by the North has reduced that number to less than 1,500 last year, and numbers thus far this year look to be even lower.

Virtually all defectors flee the North through China. Only a very few have fled across the inter-Korean border. The rare exception a few weeks ago was a North Korean soldier, who was seriously wounded as he escaped across the border. That indicates the danger as well as how uncommon it is for defectors to go directly from the North to South Korea.

For defectors who escape through China, there are other issues. China has a mixed record with Korean defectors. When relations were good between China and North Korea, most defectors who were captured in China were quickly returned to North Korea, where they were brutalized and sent to reeducation camps to discourage others from attempting to leave.

I remember one poignant conversation I had in South Korea with a young woman who fled the North and was finally able to reach the South. I asked her if this had been her first attempt. She said, "No. It was my sixth try." Five time she sought to leave, and she was captured before she reached the border in the North or after she crossed into China. She was returned to North Korean authorities and spent months each time in a reeducation camp where she was brutally treated. On her sixth attempt, she and a friend, who agreed to make another attempt with her, decided to take poison pills with them. Rather than be forcibly returned again and sent to a reeducation camp, they would have taken their own lives.

At times, when Chinese relations with South Korea have been good and China's relationship with the North was strained, the Chinese have allowed North Korea defectors to go to the South. A couple of years ago in a highly unusual arrangement, the Chinese allowed some 14 North Korean restaurant workers to fly directly from China to South Korea where they resettled.

A year or two ago, however, a THAAD missile battery was placed in the South by the U.S. with South Korean government cooperation. This led to strained relations between China and the South. Since that time, it has again been more difficult for defectors from the North to reach the South through China. I am hopeful that the recent indications of better ties between Beijing and Seoul will lead to easier conditions for defectors to pass through China.

The United States government has taken a strong interest in North Korean defectors being able to leave if they wish to do so. Although I am no longer at the Department of State, during the seven years that I was there from 2009 to early 2017, we strongly supported the South Korean effort to assist defectors to reach the South. On many occasions, I personally raised with senior Chinese government officials the U.S. concern that defectors be permitted to go to the South if that was their wish. I know that other more senior State Department officials also raised this matter with the Chinese during that time.

Mr. Chairman, it is important that the United States continue to urge China to allow defectors to resettle elsewhere. Some will wish to come to the United States, but as we have seen the number is small. If they wish to go to the South, the United States should do all we can to support South Korean efforts. Indications of Congressional support for these refugees—such as through the reauthorization of the North Korea Human Rights Act—are important, and I urge approval of that legislation. It has already been adopted by the House and is awaiting action in the Senate.

A second matter that I was asked to discuss is the issue of providing information to the people of North Korea. We must continue to encourage the free flow of information into North Korea. The availability of accurate information about events beyond the borders of the North is an extremely important in order to limit the regime's ability to manipulate its own people.

Despite the fact that it is illegal to own a radio capable of being tuned to stations other than the official government mouthpiece, we estimate, based on survey research, that as many as one third of North Koreans listen to foreign radio broadcasts. Programs from Voice of America and Radio Free Asia that are funded by Congressional appropriations are an extremely important source of information reaching the North. There are also creative and innovative programs funded by the United States to get digital information to the North Korean people. These need to be encouraged and expanded.

Mr. Chairman, military actions against North Korea are severely limited. But one thing that we can do that will encourage positive change is to increase the flow of accurate information from the outside into the North. Our human rights efforts are an important aspect of our policy toward North Korea. We must not underestimate the importance of these efforts.

Thank you very much, Mr. Chairman, for the invitation to participate in this hearing today. I look forward to any questions you and the Committee members may have.

Mr. SMITH. Thank you, Ambassador King.
Mr. Scarlatoiu.

STATEMENT OF MR. GREG SCARLATOIU, EXECUTIVE DIRECTOR, THE COMMITTEE FOR HUMAN RIGHTS IN NORTH KOREA

Mr. SCARLATOIU. Mr. Chairman, thank you for the invitation to testify before you and the subcommittee today. It is a true honor and a privilege.

The most critical challenge our country faces today is the nuclear and ballistic missile threat posed by the regime of Kim Jong-un.

Grateful for the subcommittee's unabated determination to protect North Korean refugees in China, I respectfully urge you to continue to consider the vital importance of formulating and adopting a robust human rights policy including a North Korean refugee protection policy that can be integrated into U.S. security policy toward both China and North Korea's Kim regime.

In 2014, China received a warning by the U.N. Commission of Inquiry that its policy of forcefully repatriating North Korean refugees could potentially amount to aiding and abetting North Korean perpetrators of crimes against humanity.

China has been put on notice that its policies, practices, and support for North Korea are unacceptable. Yet, at the fourth annual U.N. Security Council meeting on human rights abuses in North Korea held yesterday, China called for a procedural vote to stop the public meeting.

This effort failed but China persists in its efforts to support the Kim regime as evidenced by its forcible repatriation of North Korean refugees.

Up to 80 percent of North Korean refugees in China are women. In the absence of any semblance of protection, they fall victim to human traffickers and other criminals.

Many of those forced into sexual bondage under the guise of marriage with Chinese men in rundown rural areas are often abused by the would-be spouse and the entire family.

Their children's human security is beyond precarious. China denies North Korean children the right to education, health, and personal security as well as liberty when they are detained, awaiting forcible repatriation.

Our 2015 HRNK report, "The Hidden Gulag IV," documents the particular vulnerabilities of North Korean women jailed in a network of political prison camps—kwan-li-so—and labor camps—kyo-hwa-so.

Increasingly, these facilities house women who have attempted to flee the country and here rates of mortality, malnutrition, forced labor, and exploitation are high.

China does not uphold its obligations under international law, as evidenced by the forcible repatriation of North Korean refugees in need of protection.

China denies many North Koreans the ability to apply for asylum or have safe passage to the Republic of Korea or other countries. China claims that North Koreans are illegal economic migrants.

In reality, however, not only are North Koreans targeted for escaping the totalitarian state, but they are targeted by the Chinese Government and ultimately victimized again once repatriated to North Korea and imprisoned. It truly is a vicious cycle of political oppression and violence perpetrated against countless innocents.

Mr. Chairman, I respectfully recommend the following. First, the United States should urge China to immediately halt its forcible repatriation of North Korean refugees and thus fulfill its obligations under international treaties and customary international law.

Second, the United States should call upon China to allow the U.N. High Commission for Refugees unimpeded access to North Koreans inside China to determine whether they are refugees and whether they require assistance.

Third, the United States should call upon China to adopt legislation incorporating its international obligations under the Refugee Convention and the Convention Against Torture.

It should be expected to declare and uphold a moratorium on deportations of North Koreans until its laws and practices are brought into line with international standards.

Fourth, the United States should call upon China to recognize the legal status of North Koreans who marry or who have children with Chinese citizens and to ensure that all such children are granted resident status and access to education and other public services in accordance with both Chinese law and international standards.

Fifth, in the absence of a Chinese response the issue should be brought before international refugee and human rights fora.

UNHCR's executive committee as well as the U.N. Human Rights Council and General Assembly of the United Nations should all be expected to call on China by name to carry out its obligations under refugee and human rights law and enact legislation to codify these obligations.

Sixth, the United States should promote a multilateral approach to the problem of North Koreans leaving their country based on the principles of non-refoulement and human rights and humanitarian protection.

Building on the precedent of other refugee populations, international burden sharing should be developed to protect North Koreans seeking to escape the tyranny of the Kim regime.

Seventh, following the passage of the North Korean Human Rights Reauthorization Act of 2017, which mandates the position of the special envoy for North Korean human rights, I respectfully urge the U.S. Congress to encourage the prompt appointment of a qualified candidate.

I strongly believe that this particular issue merits the full time high-profile focus across various agencies that the special envoy has so effectively brought and would continue to bring.

And eighth, and finally, additional funds should be appropriated for clandestine information flows into North Korea, for nongovernmental organizations working to improve human rights in North Korea, and for the resettlement of North Korean refugees in the United States.

Thank you, Mr. Chairman.

[The prepared statement of Mr. Scarlatoiu follows:]

Committee for Human Rights in North Korea

1001 Connecticut Avenue, NW · Suite 435 · Washington, DC 20036 · (202) 499-7973 · www.hrnk.org

Statement of Greg Scarlatoiu, Executive Director, Committee for Human Rights in North Korea (HRNK), on "Protecting North Korean Refugees" at the Hearing of the Subcommittee on Africa, Global Health, Global Human Rights, and International Organizations, December 12, 2017

Good afternoon Chairman Smith, Ranking Member Bass, and members of the Subcommittee. Thank you for the invitation to testify before you today. It is a true honor and a privilege.

My name is Greg Scarlatoiu. I am the executive director of the Committee for Human Rights in North Korea (HRNK). We are a nonpartisan research organization headquartered in Washington, DC that conducts original research on North Korean human rights issues. Over the last 16 years, we have published over 30 reports available at HRNK.ORG, documenting for the world the horrifying truth about the extent of human rights abuses in North Korea. Our work has played a central role in assisting and informing the efforts of the US State Department, the UN Commission of Inquiry, and numerous other stakeholders who care passionately about the rights of people in North Korea. Most recently, the report submitted by UN Secretary General Antonio Guterres to the UN General Assembly on August 28th quoted one of HRNK's publications.

On behalf of HRNK, thank you for your time and interest in the plight of North Korean refugees, an ongoing human rights issue and crisis perpetuated by both North Korea and China today. The protection of North Korean refugees relates to fundamental human rights, human dignity, and state obligations under international law.

On the current situation of North Korean refugees in China

In July 2017, a North Korean refugee family of five, on their way to the Republic of Korea, committed suicide while in Chinese custody awaiting forcible repatriation to North Korea. More recently in November, reports by BBC Korea stated that China forcibly returned a group of ten refugees to North Korea, including a mother and her four-year-old son. This information comes from a Mr. Lee, the husband and father of these two victims, currently hiding in China.

For the past few years, among the interns trained at HRNK we have also worked with former North Korean refugees, currently holding South Korean citizenship. Some of these young bright escapees explained their experiences living on the run in China. One intern, when asked how she had learned Chinese, clarified that prior to her escape to South Korea, she had grown up in secret, hidden behind closed doors in China. As she was undocumented and feared the Chinese government would arrest her and forcibly return her to North Korea, her Chinese protectors brought her books to help her learn and pass the time.

China does not uphold its obligations under international law because it very rarely allows North Korean refugees access to the UN Refugee Agency (UNHCR), instead only permitting the UNHCR an office in Beijing, far from the border. As evidenced by their forcible repatriation,

Board of Directors

Katrina Lantos Swett, *Co-Chair*
Gordon Flake, *Co-Chair*
Suzanne Scholte, *Co-Vice-Chair*
John Despres, *Co-Vice-Chair*
Helen-Louise Hunter, *Secretary*
Kevin McCann, *Treasurer*

Roberta Cohen, *Co-Chair Emeritus*
Andrew Natsios, *Co-Chair Emeritus*
Morton Abramowitz
Jerome Cohen
Lisa Colacurcio
Abraham Cooper

Jack David
Debra Liang-Fenton
Nicholas Eberstadt
Carl Gershman
Jacqueline Pak
Paula Dobriansky

David Kim
Winston Lord
Steve Kahng
Marcus Noland
Greg Scarlatoiu, *Executive Director*

Committee for Human Rights in North Korea

1001 Connecticut Avenue, NW • Suite 435 • Washington, DC 20036 • (202) 499-7973 • www.hrnk.org

China denies many North Koreans the ability to apply for asylum or have safe passage to the Republic of Korea or other countries. China claims that North Koreans in need of protection are illegal economic migrants. But in reality they are victims fleeing persecution, who face a well-founded fear of persecution if forcibly returned to North Korea. Time after time we hear from North Korean refugees that when they were repatriated by China they faced imprisonment, torture, and various forms of sexual violence. Especially if the interrogators suspect that the repatriated refugees came across South Korean nationals or Christian missionaries while in China, the punishment is sure to be harsh. Determined to escape the oppression and chronic human insecurity of North Korea, some attempt to escape again, even after detention and imprisonment. Some are successful and manage to tell the stories of their harrowing escape to the outside world. Through the voices of escapees who find their way to freedom in South Korea and other countries, we know that up to eighty percent of North Korean refugees in China are women. In the absence of any semblance of protection, they fall victim to human traffickers and other criminals. Many of those forced into sexual bondage under the guise of "marriage" with Chinese men in run-down rural areas are often abused by the would-be "spouse" and the entire family. Their children's human security is beyond precarious. China denies North Korean children the right to education, health and personal security as well as liberty when they are detained awaiting forcible repatriation.

On the UN Commission of Inquiry

In 2014, the United Nations Commission of Inquiry on Human Rights in North Korea (UN COI) found that North Koreans forcibly repatriated by China systematically endure *persecution, torture while being interrogated about their activities abroad, sexual violence, and imprisonment in North Korea's inhuman detention system*. Persons found to have contact with the Republic of Korea or Christian churches may be *forcibly disappeared into political prison camps, imprisoned in forced labor camps, or summarily executed.*

The UN COI also found that North Koreans who try to flee their country and those in detention are among the primary targets of a systematic and widespread attack by North Korea, making them the most vulnerable and in need of protection. Not only are North Koreans targeted for escaping their totalitarian state, but then they are targeted by the Chinese government, and ultimately victimized again once repatriated to North Korea and imprisoned. It truly is a vicious cycle of political oppression and violence perpetrated against countless innocents.

Despite the UN COI's findings and despite the fact that North Koreans are entitled to international protection as refugees fleeing persecution or *refugees sur place*, "China pursues a rigorous policy of forcibly repatriating citizens of [North Korea] who cross the border illegally" with the view that these persons are "illegal economic migrants."

Committee for Human Rights in North Korea

1001 Connecticut Avenue, NW · Suite 435 · Washington, DC 20036 · (202) 499-7973 · www.hrnk.org

On human trafficking

Up to 90 percent of North Korean women and girls in China fall prey to traffickers in China who sell them into sexual slavery, either in forced marriages or prostitution, to their shock and horror. Countless North Korean women are victimized in this manner because they are vulnerable as they try to escape the brutal conditions of their home country. In China, the women and girls are fodder for often-rural men looking for wives. They may have arrived in China with young children too, only to be cruelly separated by human traffickers. The cycle of violence and oppression once again continues as these women and girls are held against their will or are coerced into submission out of fear that the Chinese family will report them to authorities. Additionally, impregnated women and girls by Chinese men are further victimized when the Chinese government does not recognize the children they bear as legal residents otherwise entitled to basic rights to education and other public services.

On prison camps

A core HRNK objective is to completely, verifiably, and irreversibly dismantle North Korea's vast system of unlawful imprisonment, where up to 120,000 men, women, and children are detained under abysmal circumstances, forced to work and die in prison camps because of their perceived lack of loyalty to the Kim family. As such, HRNK is aware of six operational political prison camps and the existence of over twenty potential labor camps inside North Korea, recently documented in our October 2017 report *The Parallel Gulag*.

Our 2015 report, *The Hidden Gulag IV: Gender Repression and Prison Disappearances*, documents the particular vulnerabilities of North Korean women jailed in a network of "political prison camps" (*kwan-li-so*) and "labor camps" (*kyo-hwa-so*). Increasingly, these facilities house women who have attempted to flee the country, and here, rates of mortality, malnutrition, forced labor, and exploitation are high. As our Co-Chair Emeritus Roberta Cohen, a distinguished human rights and displaced persons expert noted, "Women in particular are fleeing North Korea in ever greater numbers. When they are apprehended, they are subjected to deliberate starvation, persecution, and punishment. Their situation cries out for international attention."

In this report, we also found evidence that an additional section of Camp 12 at Jongo-ri, North Hamgyong Province, was built to imprison the influx of women arrested and forcibly repatriated by China. Our interviews with former prisoners at this camp indicate that upwards of one thousand women are enslaved here. Eighty percent, eight hundred of them, are forcibly repatriated refugees. According to our witnesses, former Camp 12 prisoners themselves, so many women prisoners were brought to the camp that a new building annex was constructed to house them. We were able to confirm the presence of the new construction through satellite imagery acquisition and analysis.

Committee for Human Rights in North Korea

1001 Connecticut Avenue, NW · Suite 435 · Washington, DC 20036 · (202) 499-7973 · www.hrnk.org

On China's non-compliance with international conventions

China received a warning by the UN COI in 2014 that its policy of forcibly repatriating North Korean refugees could potentially amount to aiding and abetting North Korean perpetrators of *crimes against humanity.* The UN COI urged China to caution relevant officials that conduct could amount to the *aiding and abetting of crimes against humanity* where **repatriations and information exchanges** are specifically directed toward or have the purpose of facilitating the commission of crimes against humanity in North Korea.

North Koreans fleeing political persecution–based on North Korea's discriminatory social class system known as *songbun*–are refugees as defined in the Refugee Convention. North Koreans with a well-founded fear of persecution upon their forcible return to North Korea by China are *refugees sur place* and must be given protection under China's international obligations, including the 1951 Convention relating to the Status of Refugees and the 1967 Protocol relating to the Status of Refugees.

China's forcible repatriation of North Korean refugees violates its obligation to uphold the principle of *non-refoulement* under the Refugee Convention. Furthermore, China violates article 3 of the Torture Convention, which states, "No State Party shall expel, return ('refouler') or extradite a person to another State where there are substantial grounds for believing that he would be in danger of being subjected to torture."

On US and global efforts to protect refugees and surge information

Notwithstanding high-level advocacy, China has forcibly repatriated tens of thousands of North Koreans. However, over 30,000 North Korean refugees now reside in over 20 nations, with the vast majority of them, 31,000 currently living in the Republic of Korea. While the United States Refugee Admissions Program remains the largest in the world, fewer than 220 refugees from North Korea have resettled since the enactment of the North Korea Human Rights Act of 2004.

As part of efforts to provide information on North Korea's human rights abuses, HRNK wrote and published a series of Wikipedia contributions on human rights in North Korea, including in Chinese. Since China is perhaps the only country in the world with substantial leverage on the Kim regime, accounting for over 80% of North Korea's foreign trade, the awareness and support of the Chinese people is now more imperative than ever, although the degree to which the public can actually influence foreign policy in China is highly debatable, to say the least. The Wikipedia pages created by HRNK are available in English, Korean, and Chinese.

On United States policy

Committee for Human Rights in North Korea

1001 Connecticut Avenue, NW · Suite 435 · Washington, DC 20036 · (202) 499-7973 · www.hrnk.org

Painfully aware of ongoing concerns and echoing HRNK's previous recommendations submitted together with then HRNK Board co-chair Roberta Cohen before a March 5, 2012 hearing of the Congressional-Executive Commission of China, I respectfully recommend the following:

First, the United States should urge China to immediately halt its forcible repatriation of North Korean refugees, and thus fulfill its obligations pursuant to the 1951 United Nations Convention relating to the Status of Refugees, the 1967 Protocol relating to the Status of Refugees, the Torture Convention, and the 1995 Agreement on the Upgrading of the UNHCR Mission in the People's Republic of China.

Second, the United States should call upon China to allow the UNHCR unimpeded access to North Koreans inside China to determine whether they are refugees and whether they require assistance.

Third, China should be called upon to adopt legislation incorporating its obligations under the Refugee Convention, the Convention against Torture, and other international human rights agreements and to bring its existing laws into line with internationally agreed upon principles. It should be expected to declare and uphold a moratorium on deportations of North Koreans until its laws and practices are brought into line with international standards.

Fourth, China should be urged to recognize the legal status of North Korean women who marry or have children with Chinese citizens, and ensure that all such children are granted resident status and access to education and other public services in accordance with both Chinese law and international standards.

Fifth, in the absence of a Chinese response, the issue should be brought before international refugee and human rights fora. UNHCR's Executive Committee as well as the UN Human Rights Council and General Assembly of the United Nations should all be expected to call on China *by name* to carry out its obligations under refugee and human rights law and enact legislation to codify these obligations so that North Koreans will not be forcibly repatriated while facing a credible fear of persecution.

Sixth, the United States should promote a multilateral approach to the problem of North Koreans leaving their country. Their exodus affects more than China. This critical issue concerns our South Korean allies most notably, as South Korea already houses 31,000 North Korean escapees, and its Constitution offers citizenship to North Koreans. Together with UNHCR, a multilateral approach should be designed that finds solutions for North Koreans based on principles of *non-refoulement* and human rights and humanitarian protection. Building on the precedent of other refugee populations, international burden sharing should be developed to protect North Koreans seeking to escape the tyranny of the Kim regime.

Seventh, following the passage of the North Korean Human Rights Reauthorization Act of 2017, which mandates the position of the Special Envoy for North Korea Human Rights, the US

Committee for Human Rights in North Korea

1001 Connecticut Avenue, NW • Suite 435 • Washington, DC 20036 • (202) 499-7973 • www.hrnk.org

Congress urge the prompt appointment of a qualified candidate. I share in the belief that the large number of special envoys in the State Department should be greatly reduced. I strongly believe, however, that this particular issue merits the full-time, high profile focus across various agencies that the Special Envoy has so effectively brought, and would continue to bring.

Eighth, that additional funds be appropriated for clandestine information flow into North Korea, for non-governmental organizations working to improve human rights in North Korea, and for the resettlement of North Korean refugees in the United States.

The most critical challenge our country faces today is the nuclear and ballistic missile threat posed by the regime of Kim Jong-un. Grateful for the Subcommittee's unabated determination to protect North Korean refugees in China, I respectfully urge you to continue to consider the vital importance of formulating and adopting a robust human rights policy, including a North Korean refugee protection policy, that can be integrated into US security policy toward both China and North Korea's Kim regime.

HRNK Resources

Four HRNK publications address the precarious plight of North Koreans in China and the cruel and inhuman practice of forcibly sending them back to one of the world's most oppressive regimes.

- The first, *The North Korean Refugee Crisis: Human Rights and International Response* (2006), edited by Stephan Haggard and Marcus Noland, establishes that most if not all North Koreans in China merit a *prima facie* claim to refugee or *refugee sur place* status. This report is available at
https://www.hrnk.org/uploads/pdfs/The_North_Korean_Refugee_Crisis.pdf.
- The second, *Lives for Sale: Personal Accounts of Women Fleeing North Korea to China* (2010), calls upon China to set up a screening process with the UN High Commissioner for Refugees (UNHCR) to determine the status of North Koreans and ensure they are not forcibly returned. This report is available at
https://www.hrnk.org/uploads/pdfs/Lives_for_Sale.pdf.
- The third, *Hidden Gulag Second Edition* by David Hawk (2012), presents the harrowing testimony of scores of North Koreans severely punished after being returned to North Korea. This report is available at
https://www.hrnk.org/uploads/pdfs/HRNK_HiddenGulag2_Web_5-18.pdf.
- The fourth, *Gender Repression and Hidden Gulag IV: Gender Repression and Prisoner Disappearances* by David Hawk (2015) finds that North Korean women, desperate to ensure their families' survival after catastrophic famine in the 1990s—are excessively victimized and detention facilities for women have notably expanded. This report, as well as satellite imagery that verifies the additional structure, are available here:
https://www.hrnk.org/uploads/pdfs/Hawk_HiddenGulag4_FINAL.pdf and
https://www.hrnk.org/uploads/pdfs/ASA_HRNK_Camp12_201608_v10_LR.pdf.

Board of Directors

Katrina Lantos Swett, *Co-Chair*	Roberta Cohen, *Co-Chair Emeritus*	Jack David	David Kim
Gordon Flake, *Co-Chair*	Andrew Natsios, *Co-Chair Emeritus*	Debra Liang-Fenton	Winston Lord
Suzanne Scholte, *Co-Vice-Chair*	Morton Abramowitz	Nicholas Eberstadt	Steve Kahng
John Despres, *Co-Vice-Chair*	Jerome Cohen	Carl Gershman	Marcus Noland
Helen-Louise Hunter, *Secretary*	Lisa Colacurcio	Jacqueline Pak	Greg Scarlatoiu, *Executive Director*
Kevin McCann, *Treasurer*	Abraham Cooper	Paula Dobriansky	

Committee for Human Rights in North Korea

1001 Connecticut Avenue, NW · Suite 435 · Washington, DC 20036 · (202) 499-7973 · www.hrnk.org

In October 2017, HRNK published *The Parallel Gulag: North Korea's "An-jeon-bu" Prisons* by David Hawk with Amanda Mortwedt Oh. The Honorable Michael Kirby, former Chair of the UN COI, states that *Parallel Gulag* "updates the record contained in the COI report" and "shows that North Korea's system of political oppression remains in place as an affront to the conscience of humanity." The report is available at https://www.hrnk.org/uploads/pdfs/Hawk_The_Parallel_Gulag_Web.pdf with picture files available at https://www.flickr.com/photos/159228385@N04/sets/72157661876737398/.

Prior Congressional testimony to the CECC on North Korean refugees by Roberta Cohen and Greg Scarlatoiu is available at https://www.hrnk.org/events/congressional-hearings-view.php?id=7 and https://www.hrnk.org/events/congressional-hearings-view.php?id=1.

Thank you for your kind consideration.

Greg Scarlatoiu
Executive Director
Committee for Human Rights in North Korea

Mr. SMITH. Thank you very much for your leadership and for that very detailed set of recommendations.

Ms. Scholte.

STATEMENT OF MS. SUZANNE SCHOLTE, PRESIDENT, DEFENSE FORUM FOUNDATION, CHAIRWOMAN, NORTH KOREA FREEDOM COALITION

Ms. SCHOLTE. First of all, I know I am going to embarrass you when I say this but I can't help it, Congressman Smith. [Laughter.]

The last time we were together there were 18 North Korean defectors in your office, and I have to tell you when we walked out of there, those defectors said, "That is the greatest man we've ever met," because you were so great to them and you have been focussing on this issue for decades.

And so I thank you so much for your leadership on this, for your bringing this hearing together today and I just wanted to say what a great, awesome person you've been.

I am also really happy to be here with Bob King, whose door was always open, who was always ready to help us when found out about a refugee that was in danger, always willing to speak out in—from small towns to college campuses and really raise the North Korean human rights profiles—issues as the special envoy for President Obama.

And also for my colleague, Greg—one of the things on my top 10 list of good things I've done in my life was insisting that he become the executive director of HRNK. So I am really glad to be with these gentleman.

So I have a very extended written testimony I've already submitted so I am going to be really brief and try to stay within the five—I think I got this down to 5 minutes 8 seconds.

So anyway, I want to make three main points. One, the situation facing North Korean refugees in China is worse than ever. Xi Jinping has brought us to a crisis stage because of his support for the regime.

Today we are relying on China to help us make sanctions effective to rein in Kim Jong-un's nuclear ambitions. But if China continues to forcefully repatriate men, women, and children back to North Korea to face certain torture, certain imprisonment, and, in some cases, execution, what does that tell us about Xi Jinping's sincerity?

The international community must insist that China and its cruel, inhumane, and illegal repatriation policy—China's policy as been—as been pointed out is a death sentence for North Koreans and as Ambassador King pointed out, 80 percent—and talked about the defectors poisoning themselves—we know 80 percent of North Korean defectors carry poison to kill themselves and we saw that dramatically happen this summer when the Korean Workers Party member, his wife, and three children committed suicide when the Chinese, on orders by Beijing, ordered them back to North Korea after they begged to be allowed to go to South Korea.

The Chinese Government continues to not only forcefully repatriate refugees but refuses to allow the UNHCR any access, but also gives free rein to North Korean agents to hunt down the refugees and those that try to help them.

We have seen the murder of Chinese citizens. We have seen the abduction of South Koreans. And what do they have in common? They have been involved in the North Korean refugee movement.

So that's the point that we've reached right now with China. China has only two choices. It can continue to support the Kim dictatorship and this will ensure an escalating nuclear arms race in Asia, which could have horrific and devastating consequences, especially for the people of Korea.

Or the other choice, which is for China to work with South Korea and the international community for peaceful unification under South Korea's democratic policies.

And I just want to give one example. The gentleman mentioned THAAD. I think both of you mentioned the THAAD.

Why did South Korea need THAAD? The only reason why South Korea needed THAAD was because of Kim Jong-un's nuclear threats, and this is an illustration of why China needs to decide whether it's going to continue to support this regime or work with South Korea and bring about the end of the Kim regime.

Second point—this is very critical, too—we need to recognize what the people of North Korea have done internally and externally to change their circumstances and support the work of the defector-led organizations.

They are our greatest allies for peaceful regime change. We all see the pictures of the goose-stepping soldiers and the fawning men and women in front of the Kim statues and we think it's a hopeless situation.

But in this great darkness of North Korea, I see the light of the North Korean people because those are the people I have been working with for over 20 years.

The reality is—we must think of this—the reality is that the people of North Korea have accomplished amazing things. It's the people externally who educated us, first of all, about the human rights tragedy—the crimes against humanity, the Kim dictatorships. But it's the people internally who are also educating themselves about the outside world.

It's the women of North Korea who internally created the market system and the ones externally who are involved the most in the rescue movement.

I know a North Korean woman who has rescued 7,000 North Koreans. I call her the Harriet Tubman of North Korea.

North Korean defectors like Park Sang-hak of Fighters for Free North Korea regularly sends in information through balloon watches and he says, "All I am doing is sending letters home about the truth."

The North Korean People's Liberation Front, men and women who served in the North Korean military, are sending in information and reaching out to the military in North Korea, citing the examples of what happened in Romania when the military sided with the people against the dictator.

Every North Korea Freedom Week we have a very emotional ceremony with the North Korean People's Liberation Front members, men and women who served in the military, raised to hate Americans, think we caused the war.

They go to the Korean War Memorial to lay a wreath and they pledge to honor the sacrifice that the Americans made for South Korea's freedom by dedicating their own lives to North Korea's freedom.

As you heard from Ms. Han from Free North Korea Radio, a radio station founded by North Korean defector Kim Sung-min and staffed by defectors, it is broadcasting every day. It is the most popular single program broadcasting into North Korea.

And one of the exciting things we do for Free North Korea Radio is create programs for them to communicate to the people of North Korea that we are not their enemy.

One program includes messages from Members of Congress in which we simply asked members to send their hopes and dreams to the people of North Korea.

The response from North Koreans to this program was absolutely amazing. During this year's North Korea Freedom Week, defectors brought portraits made of Members of Congress, including our distinguished chairman here today—Congressman Smith, and Congressman Royce, the chairman of the full committee.

These portraits were smuggled out. They were made in Pyongyang by two brothers. It took them 3 months, and the portraits came out with the message, "Tell the American politicians who deliver the messages my brother and I spent 3 months making them late into the night. Please tell them there are some people in a dark place who still have hope." And you know how beautiful—they were the most beautiful artwork I've ever seen. They shimmered.

The defectors tell us that if they had the resources to carry out their work of getting information in and out of North Korea, the regime could end in 3 years or less.

Otherwise, it could survive for another 5 to 10 years.

My third and final point, we must keep the human rights issues at the forefront, and Greg mentioned the importance of the human rights up front approach. We have to keep our concerns for the people of North Korea at the forefront, especially now—especially now with the escalating threats of Kim Jong-un.

Otherwise, we play directly into Kim's propaganda that justifies his nuclear ambitions—that we are their enemy and the enemy of the people of North Korea.

We must communicate to the people of North Korea that what the United States wants for them is to enjoy the same freedoms that South Korea Americans enjoy.

The defectors keep repeating—repeating this to us. The truth will set them free. Support the work of the defectors. Help them get the information to North Korea.

And I am presenting to you this book today called, "The Accusation." This is the only dissident book from North Korea. It was smuggled out at great risk to those involved. It was smuggled out.

It was published in English earlier this year. The author is still living in North Korea and he chose to use the pseudonym Bandi— B-A-N-D-I, Bandi—because Bandi is the Korean word for firefly. And he says he is the firefly shining a light out of the darkness of North Korea.

He's just another example of the people of North Korea who are another light shining out of this darkness. He's just another example of another North Korean risking his life just to get this message from his homeland to you.

Thank you very much.

[The prepared statement of Ms. Scholte follows:]

Suzanne Scholte, Seoul Peace Prize Laureate
President, Defense Forum Foundation; Chair, North Korea Freedom Coalition
House Committee on Foreign Affairs
Subcommittee on Africa, Global Health, Global Human Rights, and International Organizations
"Protecting North Korean Refugees" Tuesday, December 12, 2017

Thank you to Congressman Chris Smith and Congresswoman Karen Bass for your leadership on this subcommittee and bringing attention to the crisis facing North Korea refugees in China. I also want to acknowledge Congressmen Ed Royce and Eliot Engel for their leadership on the North Korea human rights issues in the Congress and the ways they have worked together in strong bi-partisan partnership to advance human rights globally.

I wish to make three main points:

-- The situation facing North Korean refugees in China is worse than ever because of Xi Jinping's illegal and inhuman repatriation policy. Xi has brought us to a crisis stage with just two options for China.

--We need to recognize what the people of North Korea have done internally and externally to change their circumstances and support the work of the defector led organizations. These defector led NGOs are our greatest weapon for peaceful regime change and the avoidance of conflict.

--We must keep the human rights issues – our concerns for the people of North Korea -- at the forefront of our policies especially now with the escalating threats by Kim Jong Un. Otherwise, we play directly into Kim's propaganda that justifies his nuclear ambitions: that we are the enemy of the people of North Korea.

Despite the fact that the world has finally come to recognize what defectors have been telling us for decades that the Kim Jong Un regime is committing crimes against humanity and gross violations of human rights, there has not been any improvement in the lives of the people of North Korea and the situation facing the refugees today is worse than ever before. There is nothing that Kim Jong Un fears more than his own people for they are the ones who have educated us about the reality of their suffering. They are the also the ones leading the efforts to change the hearts and minds of the people of North Korea.

Today, we are relying on China to help us make sanctions effective to try to reign in Kim Jong-un's nuclear ambitions, but if China continues to forcefully repatriate men, women, and children back to North Korea to face certain torture, certain imprisonment and in some cases execution, what does that tell us about Xi Jinping's sincerity?

The international community must insist that China end its cruel, inhumane, and illegal repatriation policy. North Korean defectors describe China's policy as a *"death sentence for North Koreans."* I have pointed out in previous testimony before this Committee this important fact: unlike any refugees in the world, North Korean refugees have a place to go for immediate resettlement as they are citizens of South Korea under the South Korean constitution. There is absolutely no reason for China to continue this policy.

North Korean defectors testified during this April's North Korea Freedom Week that 80% of North Korean defectors carry poison to kill themselves if they are caught by the Chinese authorities. This summer a family of five North Koreans including a senior member of the North Korea's Worker's Party, his wife, son and two daughters, were arrested by Chinese security forces. They begged them not to force them back to North Korea, but following orders from Beijing the Chinese police escorted them to the North Korean border. Fearing certain torture, imprisonment and possible execution, the family of five all committed suicide by taking poison. North Korean defectors would rather die than be repatriated to North Korea.

We saw earlier this month the desperate escape of a North Korean soldier who was shot multiple times as he fled across the DMZ to South Korea.

The Chinese government continues to refuse to allow the UN High Commissioner for Refugees any access to these refugees but gives free reign to the agents of the DPRK's Ministry of State Security to hunt down refugees and to murder those who try to help them. Even Chinese citizens have been jailed and murdered for helping North Korean refugees. Most recently we have seen the suspected abduction of a South Korean deacon Kim Won Ho in March 2016 and the murder of Chinese Pastor Han Choong-ryeol in April 2016. Both were involved in assisting North Korea refugees. These are just two examples of many cases of disappearances and suspicious deaths of those who try to assist North Korean refugees, but there are also numerous examples of Americans, South Koreans and Japanese getting arrested and imprisoned for doing something that in most countries of the world would earn acclaim: helping homeless refugees. For example, American citizens Steve Kim of New York and John Yoon of Washington served time in prison in China for helping refugees.

So, China not only forcibly repatriates North Korean refugees back to North Korean, it criminalizes those who try to assist them, and works closely with the DPRK to make the border region of China and North Korea one of the most dangerous borders in the world.

Contributing to the North Korean refugee crisis has been China's one child policy. There is a shortage of women in China. So, you have a country with a shortage of women, China, and a neighboring country, North Korea, where the women are struggling to feed their starving families, which created a horrific situation when famine struck North Korea: the trafficking of North Korean. Most North Korean females who cross that border get trafficked: sold as wives to Chinese men, sold into forced prostitution or internet pornography

And when these women are forced back to North Korea and discovered to be pregnant, the DPRK regime's policy is to force these North Korean women to undergo abortions because the babies are "half Chinese."

These decades of abuse of North Korean women in China has led to another crisis: stateless children in China, whose mothers are North Korean, and many cases of North Korean mothers being separated from their Chinese born children when they eventually are able to escape to South Korea.

We have now reached a crisis point because of Xi Jinping's support for the Kim dictatorship and there are only two choices left for China:

Continue to support the Kim dictatorship and ensure an escalating nuclear arms race in Asia which could have horrific and devastating consequences for Korea especially OR work with South Korea and the international community for peaceful unification under South Korea's leadership.

The people of China know the future is with South Korea, NOT North Korea. Even Chinese leaders and writers have expressed this view. Chinese General Wang wrote in the *Global Times* in December 2014 that *China "had cleaned up the DPRK mess too many times"* and that *"collapse is just a matter of time."* While he was editor of the *Study Times*, the journal for the Central Party School of the Communist Party of China, Deng Yuwen, wrote that China should *"give up on Pyongyang and press for the reunification of the Korean peninsula."* He lost his editorship but his words resonated. More recently he wrote: *"North Korea will ultimately fail no matter how much you throw money at it, and it is in the process of collapse."*

These Chinese leaders realize the future is with South Korea and it is time for China to stop being complicit in North Korea's crimes against humanity and end support of the Kim regime.

Just one recent example to illustrate this point: China was very much opposed to South Korea's deployment of the missile defense system, THAAD, but South Korea only felt THAAD was necessary because of Kim Jong Un's threats.

Second point, we are failing to recognize and appreciate what the people of North Korea have done through their own self determination. We need to recognize what the people of North Korea have done internally and externally to change their circumstances and support the work of the defector led organizations. These defector led NGOs are our greatest weapon for peaceful regime change and the avoidance of conflict.

We all see the pictures of the goose stepping soldiers and the fawning men and women before the Kim statues and think it is a hopeless situation. But in this great darkness of North Korea, I see the light of the people of North Korea. The reality is that the people of North Korea have accomplished amazing things making the North Korea of Kim Jong Un dramatically different than the North Korea of Kim Jong Il or Kim Il Song.

First of all, it is the people of North Korea who have educated us so that no longer can we deny that the triple Kim dictatorships have committed and are committing crimes against humanity. Over 30,000 have escaped to bear witness.

Second, it is the women of North Korea, through their own self determination, who created the market system, so that capitalism is thriving in North Korea and is why people are surviving today. Attempt after attempt by the regime to control these markets failed and the last attempt in 2009 to reassert control over the economy with a currency devaluation caused such a backlash from the people of North Korea, the regime stepped back and now allows these markets to function.

It is the people of North Korea, hungry for information and fascinated by South Korean soap operas and Western movies, that have educated themselves, so that they are far more knowledgeable about the outside world.

It is the people of North Korea who escaped who have taken up the work of saving their people and getting information into North Korea. The defectors are the ones who have been most successful in rescuing North Koreans. I know one woman, the Harriet Tubman of the North Korean underground railroad, who has rescued 7000 people from her homeland.

Defectors have also taken up the work that we use to do of getting information into North Korea. For example, Park Sang Hak of Fighters for Free North Korea regularly sends in leaflets of information, shortwave radios, usbs, and money for the markets via balloon launches. Park's messages include true information about South Korea, true history, and important news. He states: "All I am doing is sending letters home about the truth." His most recent balloon launches informed the people of North Korea that Kim Jong Un murdered his own half brother and also told them about the murder of Otto Warmbier, so that North Koreans would know about these horrible crimes.

It is defectors like Choi Jeong Un, Choi Joo Hwal, and Cha Ri-hyuk of the North Korea People's Liberation Front who have sent in 12,000 notels, 400 shortwave radios and 50,000 USBs with information, and batteries. Because the electricity situation is dire, they are also smuggling in batteries for the notels and the radios.

They are especially reaching out to the military in North Korea. They are sharing with them the history of what happened in Rumania when the military sided with the people against the dictator and ended the dictatorship there and calling for them to do that for North Koreans.

Every North Korea Freedom Week begins with a very emotional ceremony led by the North Korea People's Liberation Front, men and women who served in the North Korea military. Having been raised to hate Americans and believe that we caused the Korean War, these former North Korean soldiers go to the Korean War Memorial and lay a wreath and pledge to honor the sacrifice Americans made for South Korea's freedom by dedicating themselves to North Korea's freedom.

Another defector organization is Free North Korea Radio, which is broadcasting every day into North Korea and can be heard throughout North Korea and the border region in China. It is staffed by North Korean defectors and was founded by Kim Seong Min, a former DPRK Army captain.

The greatest weapon we have in dealing with North Korea is the truth and the best tellers of the truth are the defectors who have escaped. I will give you several clear examples that prove this point.

During North Korea Freedom Week 2015 defectors wrote a declaration stating: *"We are North Korean defectors who left parents, siblings, and other family behind in North Korea. Those we love are still in North Korea, and because we know better than anyone how they are living we are working for the rights of the North Korean people...Our goals are to make North Korean society a democracy and a reunified Korea a country that can play a role in spreading peace throughout the world, starting in East Asia."*

In August 2015 when two South Korean soldiers were maimed by land mines planted by the North Korean military, South Korea decided to turn the loud speakers back on at the DMZ that had been silenced since the Sunshine Policy. For three days, they played *K-Pop music*, and regular South Korean news programming. But on the fourth day the South Korean government -- on those loud speakers – started broadcasting the programs of Free North Korea Radio. What happened next: North Korea immediately demanded to go back to the negotiating table. During the September 2015 negotiations, North Korea did not ask for a peace treaty, which they always are asking for; North Korea did not ask for the end of ROK-US military exercises, which they are always asking for. North Korea only asked for one thing during the September 2015 negotiation and that was: "Turn off the loud speakers." The North Korea regime could not have their soldiers and citizens hear the voices of their brothers and sisters living in freedom in South Korea.

One of the exciting things we do is provide special programs for Free North Korea Radio to help them communicate to the people of North Korea that we are not their enemy, and we certainly do not "occupy South Korea" as they are brainwashed to believe. In fact, the friendship between America and South Korea is what helped propel South Korea into the 11th largest economy in the world.

One of the programs we started a few years ago is to send messages to North Korea from American leaders during Seollal (Korean New Year) and on August 15th (Korean Liberation Day). We asked Members of the U.S. Congress to send us messages of what they would like to say to the PEOPLE of North Korea, to share their hopes and dreams. Our hope was to show through your words how much the American people care about the people of North Korea. These messages were powerful, and the response from North Korea was amazing from the radio station's informants.

One man in North Korea reported *"The [North Korean] government always mentions that America is our total enemy but a lot of people already know that America is the most developed and democratic country...I never imagined that politicians from the U.S. would have participated in the radio show, which is run by North Korean defectors, and send messages to North Koreans."*

Another citizen said *"We never dare to say Kim Jung Eun's government should be collapsed, so that people can live peacefully. However, I am extremely happy that someone else could say this for us."*

During this past April's North Korea Freedom Week the defectors brought with them something truly amazing: Hand woven silk portraits made of three Members of Congress by two brothers living in Pyongyang who listen to Free North Korea Radio. If they had been caught doing this, they would have been executed. The portraits were smuggled out with this message: *"Tell the American politicians who delivered the messages. My brother and I spent three months making them late into the night. Please tell them there are some people in a dark place who still have hope because of South Korea and the US."*
One other indicator of the importance of this work is see who is on Kim Jong Un's assassination list: this list tells you who he fears most. Number one on the list is Kim Seong Min, the founder and director of Free North Korea Radio, and number two is Park Sang Hak, the founder and director of Fighters for Free North Korea.

The defectors tell us that if they had the resources to carry out their programs getting information in and out of North Korea the regime could end in three years or less; otherwise it could survive for another five to ten years. Balloon launches, radio broadcasting, smuggling in USBs, Notels, utilizing drones, which is the newest method being utilized, are ALL critical because of the different ways to reach people in the different regions of North Korea.

Finally third and last point, we must keep the human rights issues – our concerns for the people of North Korea -- at the forefront of our policies especially now with the escalating threats by Kim Jong Un. Otherwise, we play directly into Kim's propaganda that justifies his nuclear ambitions: that we are the enemy of the people of North Korea. We must communicate to the people of North Korea that what the United States wants for them is to enjoy the same freedoms that South Koreans and Americans enjoy.

We need to emphasize that the friendship with the United States and the freedoms in South Korea are what led South Korea, out of the ashes and devastation of the Korean War, to become in a relatively short period the 11th largest economy in the world. When we fail to put human rights at the forefront and focus exclusively on the nuclear issue we feed into the lie that Kim Jong Un tells the people of North Korea: we are their enemy and want to destroy them and therefore North Korea must have nuclear weapons.

For example, the speech that President Donald Trump gave in Seoul was exactly the right message. I have worked on North Korea human rights issues for over 20 years and that was the best speech any American -- or South Korean -- President has ever given about what our brothers and sisters in North Korea have suffered under the triple Kim dictatorships.

During North Korea Freedom Week, the defectors kept repeating: *the truth will set them free. the truth will set them free. Help us get the truth to North Korea.* To underscore these points, I have brought with me further proof about the importance of the people of North Korea. I am presenting to you this book *The Accusation* – the only dissident book from North Korea. It was smuggled out of North Korea and published in English earlier this year. The author is still living in North Korea and he chose to use the pseudonym, Bandi. Bandi is Korean for Firefly as he is the Firefly shining a light out of the darkness of North Korea.

He is just another example of the amazing spirit of the people of North Korea, the light shining out of the darkness, another North Korean risking his life just to get you his message from his homeland to you. Thank you.   ###

Mr. SMITH. Ms. Scholte, thank you very much for your extraordinary leadership over the course of over two decades. It really has made a difference.

I do have a number of questions but I'll try to keep them a little bit brief. If any of you would like to speak to the issue of the cult of personality, which I think is grossly underappreciated by the Pentagon and by many of the people within our own military.

We know that when people believe that they are serving a god—in this case, a demigod, someone who is actually doing horrific things but claiming to be God—certainly, his grandfather did—that the sense of extremism and obsession almost knows no bounds.

I know a lot of Americans, when they see documentary footage of people crying so profusely they think it's orchestrated, people tell me, including experts like yourselves, it's not.

They really do—okay, they can gin some of that up but so much of it is from the earliest years inculcated into the minds and hearts.

And I did ask our two previous witnesses, how do they break free of that, and the truth does set you free but it has to be applied over time which is why broadcasting and other means of communication are so important.

But if you could speak to that whole issue of Juche. I've read one book about it by a Christian who said you've got to understand why they are so fanatical and why they will die in large numbers for Kim, whoever the Kim might be at that time, which we, again, under appreciate. The sense being able to reason effectively goes out the window.

So I just ask you if you could speak to that first and then I'll get to some other questions.

Mr. SCARLATOIU. Yes, Mr. Chairman.

Indoctrination begins at a very early age in North Korea. It begins at the precognizant age. Babies in the cradle are taught to point fingers to the pictures of Kim Il-song and Kim Jong-il on the wall.

Laws are on paper. North Korea has a constitution that even provides for freedom of religion and freedom of expression, labor legislation, a criminal code.

But in practice, none of these laws are applied. North Koreans do not know the international obligations that North Korea has assumed by ratifying, for example, the International Covenant on Civil and Political Rights, the International Covenant on Economic, Social, and Cultural Rights or their own legislation.

The only principles that govern each and every aspect of life in North Korea are the Ten Principles of Monolithic Ideology as evidenced in our recent research and publications by Robert Collins. Each and every North Korean has to participate in weekly ideological training sessions, self-criticism sessions.

This is very much part of life. During those long years that all men and many women spend in the military, indoctrination is taken to the next stage. One has, of course, to remember that the age of revolution in Budapest 1956, Prague 1968, or Bucharest 1989 was late teens, early 20s, mid-20s.

That's the age when each and every North Korean man is in a military uniform. By the time they are done the age of revolution has passed.

Juche—of course, this is North Korea's self-reliance ideology. On the surface, it sounds very different from Marxism. Marxism basically preaches that ownership of the means of production is the main driver of history. Juche claims that the individual is the main driver of history.

We had a senior fellow—resident senior fellow, very nice lady, born and raised in North Korea. She used to be a professor of Juche thought in North Korea. Now she's a university professor in South Korea.

She would tell us every time we asked her about Juche, don't worry about Juche. The only—the sole purpose of Juche is to worship the leader, to solidify the leader's personality cult.

Basically, the individual makes sense, individual life only makes sense for as long as it's lived as part of the commonwealth. Life makes sense only if it's lived for the sake of the Supreme Leader.

As to information campaigns, the critical information campaigns that we launched into North Korea must surely be cognizant and fully knowledgeable of the different cognitive processes in North Korea.

We must be fully cognizant that education is very different. World views are very different. The way North Koreans approach ideas is very different. So we are much better off if we have former North Koreans in charge of working on content and delivering this content perhaps in collaboration with other organizations. But they must definitely be involved in this process.

Mr. KING. Mr. Chairman, one of the things that I think we need to be careful about is that I am not sure the North Koreans are as indoctrinated as we would sometimes think.

Barbara Demick, in her book, "Nothing to Envy," talks about what life was like in North Korea. One of the very telling incidents she cites is about a particular family and how they dealt with the death of Kim Il-sung in 1994.

The mother told the daughter, "At school today you're going to have a memorial service for Kim Il-sung. You have to cry. You must have real tears. If you can't cry, spit in your hand and wipe it on your eyes so that everyone will know that you're crying."

They understand and they can see that. It's a society where to deviate becomes so difficult that people who may have different views or see things differently don't talk about it because of the nature of the society.

I think this is not a place where you've got to convince people that other things are true. This is a place where people need to have an opportunity to do that.

The key thing is making sure that we get information into North Korea that provides an alternative explanation of what's going on in the world and that, again, is the importance of news broadcasting and information dissemination.

That is where we need to make sure that there is funding for Voice of America, Radio Free Asia, and for the programs that are being developed to do that.

Mr. SMITH. Ms. Scholte.

Ms. SCHOLTE. Well, first of all, I just want to tell you, I totally agree with you that this—the understanding of the Juche ideology is something that is completely under appreciated.

The—one of the witnesses we had during North Korea Freedom Week this last year was from Pyongyang. She was part of the elites. She and her mom ran a restaurant, had the good life.

She was—she said that when Kim Jong-il died, they thought they were all going to die, and I think maybe the Juche police system is probably more powerful in Pyongyang because it's the elites that are there and they are not—and they are more—actually more isolated than people, like, for example, in the border regions.

But I think it's a very important controlling system in the brain, with the brainwashing from the start. But it's really focused on the fact that the Kim family are God and Juche has really become the worship.

Not the self-reliance that Hwang Jang-yop, who's the author of Juche, established but the worship of the Kim dictatorship.

And Hwang Jang-yop interestingly pointed out when he defected, he said the way to break the Juche ideology is with the Holy Spirit. He actually became a Christian before he died, and he was really involved with Free North Korea Radio and Ms. Han cited the programs where they—these are programs that are—that are done to worship the regime, the songs—I am sorry, the songs that are meant.

They changed the wordings of the songs. And Greg mentioned the importance of the messaging. That's exactly the kind of thing to change to address that belief system directly with truthful information, and this is one of the clever ways that the North Koreans are being able to do it.

But I do think it's very important that we realize the cult of personality that's part of this Juche and the brainwashing that starts from the very moment they are children when they—even math problems—"how many American GIs did you kill when you threw a grenade."

I mean, this starts at the very beginning. We need to be aware of that.

And I'll finally say that the first defectors we brought over, one was an army captain. It was back in 1997, an army captain and a colonel, and they got up in front of the audience and said, "None of you guys look like wolves and your noses are a lot smaller than I thought they were going to be" because all Americans are supposed to have these long crooked noses. But it's just part of that brainwashing that we need to be aware of and that's why getting information is so important.

Mr. SMITH. Mr. Scarlatoiu, you underscored that up to 90 percent of the North Korean women and girls in China fall prey to traffickers in China who sell them into sexual slavery.

As you might know, I am the prime author of the Trafficking Victims Protection Act and I tried for years to get China designated as a Tier 3 country, an egregious violator, in part because of the exploding sex trafficking within mainland China but also in large part too because of so many North Koreans who were so horrifically abused.

And, again, Ms. Scholte provided us with several witnesses over the course of several hearings who were themselves trafficked and told their stories again before this committee.

This year, the Trump administration has designated China Tier 3, and in the narrative explaining that, great focus is put on this trafficking problem.

They are not in freedom. They are in another kind of slavery that they are trying to escape from in North Korea.

So my question would be, because we do have votes now so I am going to ask a number of questions so that we can finish before the voting is over, but if you could speak to that.

We are at the sanctions part now. Tier 3 has been designated. At the time and place—anytime, any day now, the administration could announce a series of sanctions toward China.

What would you recommend that we do? There is a lot on the plate that could be imposed and I think a designation without a sanction weakens the designation significantly.

Secondly, on the issue of refoulement, which you spoke to in your testimony, we know that the periodic review is coming up in November 2018 under the Refugee Convention.

NGOs can begin submitting in the spring. But it seems to me, this ought to be an engraved invitation for every one of us to make China—China's sending people back to death—they are taking poison to avoid it—and certainly to torture and mistreatment in the gulag system.

This is an opportunity to begin even right now, and your thoughts on that. And, of course, there are some—under customary international law there are other obligations to which China is obliged to. Any thoughts along those lines?

There was a report today of five refugee camps—you heard it earlier mentioned to our two previous witnesses. Is that because China thinks something is going to happen vis-a-vis a war? Or is this just another modality of control that they are seeking to impose?

The ICC, unfortunately, has had a very checkered—two convictions in 14 years. The International Criminal Court has not been that robust. But it seems to me, as you have been saying, and as the U.N. Commission has found, or at least would lead us to believe, when you're complicit in these crimes you're complicit, and it would seem to me that not just North Korea but the prosecutors should be looking at China's complicity in this terrible death spiral that they are on now.

So if you could speak to that. I have many other questions but we will run out of time, so please.

Mr. SCARLATOIU. Mr. Chairman, certainly, there is ample evidence of the abuse that has affected North Korean women in China for more than two decades now.

We have to take that leap—link China directly to the egregious human rights violations affecting North Koreans and in particular affecting North Korean refugees.

Perhaps we need to take a hard look at certain areas, certain industries, certain areas of the economy that are more closely related to this issue of North Korean refugees in China—the lack of protection, the vulnerability of these refugees, China's refoulement of

North Korean refugees—take a very hard look at areas that could be perhaps subjected to sanctions.

In—as far as the refoulement issue is concerned, we often hear the question as to why China is so reluctant to provide protection to these North Korean refugees.

I would take the liberty of sharing a thought with you. Perhaps China is afraid of a development similar to the European picnic of the summer of 1989 when Hungary opened its border to East Germans and this outflow of East Germans out of East Germany was one of the fundamental factors that ultimately brought about the fall of the Berlin Wall.

Clearly, if there is one step that China can take to make a huge difference—a very significant difference, that would be to stop the forcible repatriation of North Korean refugees.

The International Criminal Court—the referral of the Kim regime by the U.N. Security Council to the International Criminal Court was one of the fundamental recommendations made in the February 2014 report of the U.N. Commission of Inquiry. North Korea is not a party to the International Criminal Court.

Of course, the problem with the Security Council is that the P5 members—the permanent members—have veto power and China is one of them. The Russian Federation is, of course, another one.

So we face the prospect of a Chinese or Russian veto. Where we are right now is that for a fourth time yesterday, the North Korean human rights issue was placed on the agenda of the U.N. Security Council.

Now, placing the issue on the agenda is a procedural matter that requires nine out of 15 votes of permanent and nonpermanent members. Once the issue is taken up, it becomes substantive and it becomes subject to a veto by one of the P5 members.

Another possibility that has been raised by international human rights NGOs is the creation of a special tribunal through the General Assembly.

The tool kit of accountability is a complex one and pursuing the avenue of the International Criminal Court is just one of many avenues we can consider.

Mr. KING. You raised an interesting question about dealing with the Tier 3 sanctions on China. The difficulty of looking at sanctions as the key on these issues with the North Koreans is that, again, we are in a situation where we are trying to get the Chinese to solve the North Korean problem for us because we have such limited abilities to do it.

This is our problem with sanctions on the nuclear weapons and we are going to be in trouble if we take that same route on human rights.

There is a real link between sanctions on trafficking and repatriation. The reason why these women are trafficked is because they will be repatriated if they don't have some way to hide their presence there.

And if we can move the Chinese in a direction where they allow the North Korean refugees to leave China, we don't have to worry about sanctions for trafficking because there won't be a trafficking problem. These women will leave. I think we need to sort of look at it in a way that will allow us to work with the Chinese and try to put some pressure on them to make some progress on repatriation rather than saying, you know, let's slap more sanctions on the Chinese.

It's an issue that's not easy. It's an issue that's complicated. But it's an issue that's connected and we need to figure out how to do it.

And I think that's the difficulty of dealing with China. We don't like what the Chinese do. We don't like their human rights record. We don't like their obstacles in dealing with the North Korean human rights issue or the North Korean nuclear issue.

The argument has been we are probably better to try to work with the Chinese because they are suffering from the same problem and if we can work with them maybe we will have some progress.

It is helpful to have the threat of sanctions because it's very clear that the sanctions on nuclear weapons are successful because the Chinese are beginning to enforce them. The Chinese are beginning to enforce them because we have imposed sanctions on the Chinese for not enforcing them.

So we need to balance that process out. But I think we need to focus U.S. Government policy not just on the nuclear weapons issue but also on the human rights issue because that's the key to opening up North Korea.

Mr. SMITH. Before I go to Ms. Scholte, Andrew Natsios testified before our subcommittee a couple years ago and that was precisely his major point—that we have delinked human rights from the nuclear issue in the same way we did it with Iran. And when—if it's a sidebar issue or something that's done out in the hallway, it doesn't get done.

And when we fail, as we have failed, unfortunately, on the nuclear side, what do you have to show for it? People's human rights have not been advanced——

Mr. KING. Exactly. That's why we need a special envoy for North Korea human rights to make sure that that is part of the discussion. Yes.

Ms. SCHOLTE. Well, for bringing up sanctions, I did want to say one thing about North Korea sanctions, which has been reported because you brought up the topic of sanctions, Free North Korea Radio and other entities have reported that the people of North Korea—one of the big worries that we all had with the sanctions against North Korea is not wanting to hurt the people of North Korea—that it be very carefully targeted at Kim Jong-un and the elites.

And what we are hearing now is not only have the sanctions not hurt the people of North Korea but they are actually doing better, that the—because there is products that they can't export that they are having to dump on the North Koreans.

So all these costs have gone down. So I wanted to talk about that. But on the sanctions regarding China, first of all, I want to start out by saying this.

I think we have really failed the people of China and I hope that we don't continue to fail the people of North Korea.

But I think we have really failed the people of China because we have turned back on the many horrific human rights violations that are happening against the people of China at all different lev-

58

els, and this has been going on for decades for all our, I would say, economic greed.

And I would cite two experts on this. Dr. Greg Autry, the professor who wrote the book "Death by China" and explores the intellectual property theft and the things that the Chinese—and I am talking very specifically about the regime in China—have done and profited at the expense of the American people, and also Dr. Yang Jianli, who I know you have—who has been just an amazing leader in the Chinese human rights movement. But we have not—we have betrayed people like them that are fighting for the human rights of the people of China as well.

And so I think any kind of sanctions or pressure on the Xi Jinping regime is critically important. He is culpable. He is committing crimes against humanity.

And on the refugee camps, that was the rumors we have been hearing off and on for decades. Why would we need refugee camps? Just let the UNHCR go in there and start letting these people go.

And I remember one time when there was a planeload of North Koreans that the Chinese allowed leave. It was in the summer because I remember I was on vacation. It was probably, like, 10 years ago.

But they let a planeload go and RFA called me up, tracked me down on vacation and said, "Suzanne, Suzanne, do you think the Chinese are changing their policy? They are letting a whole planeload of North Koreans back to South Korea." And I said, "Not unless the planes keep flying," and there were not any more flights.

So I am not sure about these refugee camps. There is not a need for one. North Koreans are the only refugees in the world that have a place to go for immediate resettlement because they are citizens of South Korea under Article 2 of the South Korean constitution.

They are unlike any refugees in the world. And I know we have a refugee crisis going on because of tensions in the Middle East and North Africa. But North Koreans don't—we have Hanawon, that's the refugee camp.

Finally, on China fearing refugees, here's the thing. If China fears being overwhelmed by refugees if it showed some compassion, all it's doing is lifting off the pressure on Kim Jong-un that's causing all the tensions to begin with and relieving him of any reason to reform so that people don't want to leave.

Talk to North Koreans. They don't want to leave their homeland. They love their homeland. They are only leaving because of the horrific human rights violations of a dictator there.

So what China is doing is prolonging the dictatorship by forcing them back and being complicit in crimes against humanity.

And I think that more and more Chinese are recognizing this. They are speaking out that the future is with South Korea. I believe that China fears having a strong unified democracy on its border and that's the reason why they are continuing to send the refugees back. They just don't want to see a Korea unified.

I always point out that if the regime collapsed there is not going to be any refugee problem. The thing you're going to have to control is people trying to go there. And I always tease the pastors from—because the pastors, the Methodists and the Presbyterians, are going to be fighting to plant their churches there.

Hyundai and everybody else is going to be going there to build plants. All the Korean Americans are going to be going home because that's their ancestral homeland—and the real fear is—what we will have to be concerned about is protecting the development in North Korea and protecting the North Korean people once that regime is gone from the flood of people coming in.

Mr. SMITH. Thank you.

We have heard instances of U.N. agencies approving technology transfers to North Korea in violation of U.N. sanctions and the World Intellectual Property Organization—WIPO—has had problems with that, and we have raised them.

I actually had a hearing in February 2016 on that. We have written letters. It's come to very little outcome. Your thoughts on that?

It seems to me that for sanctions to work it's not just the countries but it's also U.N. agencies that need to be in compliance. Your thoughts?

Mr. SCARLATOIU. Chairman Smith, I believe you are referring to an agent called Tabun that the North Koreans were actually licensed to produce. It's one component needed in the production of chemical weapons, I believe.

Our organization, the Committee for Human Rights in North Korea, has focused more on the humanitarian arm of the U.N. and one point that we have tried to make time and time again is that U.N. agencies involved in humanitarian operations inside North Korea should be fully cognizant of human rights concerns, of the U.N. Commission of Inquiry report, the recommendations of the U.N. Commission of Inquiry and apply a human rights up front approach to their work.

And I will take the liberty of giving a very quick example. Last year, we documented Prison Camp Number 12 in Chongo-ri, North Hamgyong Province. In the aftermath of Typhoon Lionrock the U.N. was conducting a fact finding mission in the vicinity of the camp.

We managed to acquire satellite images through the cloud cover proving that the camp had been affected by the flooding caused by Typhoon Lionrock.

We urged U.N. agencies to include the most vulnerable segments of the population, especially prisoners, in the fact finding missions and humanitarian operations in North Korea.

For example, the World Health Organization has a program called Health in Prisons applied throughout the developing world. Why not seek ways to apply some of these programs to North Korea?

One positive aspect here, although action on the ground is lacking is that senior U.N. officials were very responsive, including, at the time, the Deputy Secretary General, and in his most recent report that U.N. Special Rapporteur on North Korean human rights, on human rights in the DPRK. Mr. Thomas Ojea Quintana did specifically mention the need to address the most vulnerable in North Korea including prisoners.

Mr. KING. Thank you for what you did, having a hearing to focus on the U.N. problem. U.N. agencies are like any big bureaucracy where you have people who aren't aware of what is going on in other places.

They are, however, very attentive to what the U.S. Congress has to say and I think your efforts are extremely useful in dealing with these kind of problems with U.N. agencies not being aware of sanctions and so forth.

Thank you.

Ms. SCHOLTE. Ditto.

Mr. SMITH. Ms. Scholte, you said it's worse now under Xi Jinping. Ms. Hee said it's worse under Kim Jong-un. It seems like it's been worsening since 2011.

Dr. King, if I could go back to your testimony where you said it reached a high. Now it's gone down. It's less than 1,500 last year. It could be even worse this year.

How much worse can it get before the Security Council—well, they may never do it because of the veto. But I am a great believer in hybrid courts.

I've been pushing for 4 years that there be a special court for Syria and Iraq. Got a resolution passed. Had a series of hearings on it.

We had the former prosecutor for Sierra Leone testify at two of those hearings and, of course, they put Charles Taylor behind bars for 50 years. So, it shows that hybrid courts get results.

There are imperfections but they do get results. The ICC often doesn't. So I think your point was well taken, Mr. Scarlatiou.

There are other alternatives and they have been put on the table. I think we should pursue that aggressively. We still may run into the Security Council problem. But even the effort might have some mitigating effect on the Chinese barbaric behavior and, of course, the parallel barbaric behavior by the North Korean Government. Your thoughts on that?

Mr. KING. The International Bar Association held a proceeding a couple weeks ago looking at what information there is about crimes against humanity being committed in North Korea.

They concluded that there is sufficient solid evidence on 10 of 11 crimes against humanity to hold individuals in North Korea responsible.

I think we need to focus on this idea of accountability. I think we need to go as far as we can. I think it's useful to have the Security Council debating and discussing the human rights situation in North Korea.

Even if we aren't going to get a vote out of the Security Council, it raises the issue to that level. It puts pressure on the North Koreans and we need to continue that effort. I think what you were trying to do with Syria is something that would be worth trying to do with North Korea.

Ms. SCHOLTE. I just—I met a young woman who escaped with her 14-year-old daughter. This was about 7 years ago. And she told me that when her 14-year-old daughter got repatriated—they got—they got to China, they got arrested. Her 14-year-old daughter got—they got separated.

The 14-year-old daughter got repatriated and beaten to death by a border guard. And when I heard that story, I was so horrified. How could any man beat a 14-year-old girl who was simply trying to have a better life?

But at that point, I started pushing the South Korean Government to convene a tribunal because at that point the South Korean Human Rights Commission had already collected 532 cases of these types of abuses where—and the people knew, gave testimonies.

But when they put that report together they never released the names, and I think one thing was really encouraging that Ambassador King was involved with during President Obama's administration was starting to name names—naming names of the perpetrators of these crimes, which I think is so important.

We are part of the U.N. Commission—I am sorry, the U.N. Commission of Inquiry that's pushing for the ICC referral.

However, we can't wait, and even if he gets prosecuted at the ICC and the ICC determines he was committing crimes against humanity, well, he could still be dictator.

It might not have any impact. So we have got to look at other ways and I've always believed that hybrid court, whatever, there has to be a procedure to start talking about these issues because I think we need to put people in the regime on notice.

They've got to wake up every morning, the people that are keeping this regime going—they have to wake up every morning with two choices: Total devotion and loyalty to Kim Jong-un or having their brains splattered along with their family by anti-aircraft weaponry. I mean, that's what they face every day.

So how do you get that to stop? You've got to tell them, "You're going to be held accountable for your crimes." But at the same time, you've got to reach out to them through programs like Freedom North Korea, through the defectors, because there are defector elites who are reaching out to other elites and showing them that there is another alternative—there is another option.

But I think proceeding on these kinds of legal courts is absolutely critical to put pressure on them to show them they are going to be held accountable.

There has to be a way to stop that border guard from beating to death a 14-year-old girl when his name gets mentioned in a South Korean tribunal. But also Bob cited the International Bar Association. They did release their report this morning, which found that the crimes against humanity meaning that almost every single statute—there was just one they were lacking the evidence. But the evidence is there of the crime against humanity being committed by Kim.

Mr. SMITH. Let me ask you, and maybe it'll be the last question. You've been very generous with your time. How would you rate the effectiveness of the Human Rights Council toward China?

I remember when it was called the Human Rights Commission. I traveled frequently to Geneva, would try to lobby people on particular issues including China. I actually went to a China press conference and asked some questions about human rights and they shut it down.

They were so unwilling and so brittle when it comes to criticism. They just ended the press conference because they didn't want to answer serious questions about human rights.

I've met with Prince Zeid, the high commissioner for human rights. I am deeply disappointed, and I would appreciate your thoughts, one way or the other. Maybe you think he's doing a good job.

When it comes to Israel they are obsessed with holding Israel to account for things, for instance, settlements. Security Council Resolution 2334 makes it criminal—illegal for certain settlements, and Abbas is now petitioning the ICC to open up a case for prosecution.

Are you kidding me? Then you have gross violations of human rights being committed every day with complicity by the Chinese but also with complicity with the Chinese. And, there is very little—a statement made here or there but it's never offensive in terms of trying to hold them accountable.

I think it makes the credibility of the Human Rights Commission suspect. They cannot be politicized. We know that there are rogue nations who make a beeline to sit on the council in order to run interference to their own accountability being held and they work in tandem with each other to keep the rogue nations not focused upon.

So if you could speak to that and particularly to Prince Zeid, because his black list is coming out very shortly of companies doing business with entities in what they falsely call occupied territory, and I say falsely because I believe it's false.

But it's a very, very bad omen, I think, for the council to be so politicized and then look askance when it comes to China.

Your thoughts?

Mr. KING. There is nothing more frustrating than trying to deal with the Human Rights Council. On the one hand, they have a very high-minded goal and objective. On the other hand, the realities of politics are constantly getting in the way.

Israel is one of the most troubling of issues because the votes are in the wrong place and it becomes a very difficult problem.

The one bright light with the Human Rights Council is the treatment of North Korea. North Korea has not sat on the Human Rights Council; it has never been elected a member of the council.

North Korea has gone through the Universal Periodic Review process. They've been under some pressure because of that process and there have been some indications of improvement in non-controversial areas like assistance for people with disabilities and that kind of thing.

We have been able to get out of the Human Rights Council every year since 2004 a tough strong resolution that is critical of North Korea. We have been able to refer things to the General Assembly. We have been able to get tough strong resolutions.

As far as North Korea Policy is concerned, the Human Rights Council is a good instrument. As far as Israel is concerned, it's not. [Laughter.]

Mr. SMITH. I mean, even today, December 11th, Prince Zeid has called for North Korea to be referred to the ICC.

Mr. KING. Yes.

Mr. SMITH. That is easy lift. That's not all that hard to say that.

Mr. KING. No. [Laughter.]

Mr. SMITH. But what about its accomplice, China? And I appreciate your thoughts, too.

Mr. KING. The issue with China is more complicated. China is a permanent member. It can veto anything of substance in the Security Council.

Mr. SMITH. But his recommendation—I mean, they can reject it——

Mr. KING. Yes.

Mr. SMITH [continuing]. But the credibility and gravitas that the high commissioner would bring to saying, "Hey, you too, China."

Mr. KING. Yes.

Mr. SMITH. "We are not letting you off the hook. You are complicit in these horrific crimes."

Mr. KING. Yes. It's a tough one. You're a politician. These countries are dealing with politics. We are making progress. We are not there yet.

I think we need to continue the effort and we need to continue to criticize—the way you and other colleagues in Congress have done—to put pressure on the U.N. agencies for what they are not doing.

But I think we should also be careful not to throw the baby out with the bath. Praise them for what they've done in areas like what they've done on North Korea. I think we have made real progress on that.

Mr. SMITH. Before we go to Greg, we ought to remind everyone and begin assembling lists. We just recently passed the Frank Wolf International Religious Freedom Act. I did sponsor it, and it calls for designated persons, people that we can hold to account.

The Magnitsky Act and, certainly, the Global Magnitsky Act gives us an incredible tool on a vast array of human rights issues to say so and so, so and so, so and so, and begin honing in on the individuals who commit atrocities all over the world.

We got the CPC designation, both China and North Korea, under the Religious Freedom Act. So sanctions can be levied there. And then, of course we know that, we have the Trafficking Victims Protection Act sanctions, Tier 3, where they can be levied there as well.

So we have got all these tools. Let's use them.

Please, Greg.

Mr. SCARLATOIU. I fully agree with Ambassador King that there is serious tension between the lofty goals, ideals, and principles and standards that the U.N. Human Rights Council is supposed to uphold and the politicization of the council.

It's highly politicized, of course, as a human rights NGO dealing with the U.N. and U.N. agencies. My colleagues and board members know that it's extraordinarily frustrating many times—most of the time to deal with U.N. agencies and yet, as Ambassador King said, if there is one success story of the U.N. Human Rights Council that was the establishment of the U.N. Commission of Inquiry through a resolution that didn't even go to a vote. It was passed by consensus by all 47 members of the Human Rights Council.

So North Korea is, after all, the saving grace of the Human Rights Council, if I may say so, and we do hope to continue to see good action on North Korean human rights issues.

Mr. SMITH. Ms. Scholte.

Ms. SCHOLTE. Yes. I think we need tremendous reform at the U.N. I think it's, in some cases, it's a joke. The Human Rights Council—why can't we have a Human Rights Council where the membership is based on the countries observing the Universal Declaration of Human Rights—just a few of them?

I mean, let's reestablish what the Universal Declaration of Human Rights stood for and let's have, you know, you can be on the Human Rights Council if your country, well, maybe—maybe at least 60 percent.

How about just 60 percent, and I'll give you a D minus to be on the council. It's ridiculous what's happening. And while it's a bright light on North Korea, I am not sure that it's done anything. It's done nothing, actually, to improve the lives of the people of North Korea.

The lives of the people of North Korea have not improved. We just know more about it. That's all that's happened. We just know how much they are suffering. The reality is it's because of the people of North Korea, not because of the dictatorship and certainly not because of anything that the U.N. has done. So it may be a good mouthpiece on North Korea but it's failing on the human rights and suffering of so many other people.

Mr. SMITH. You know, I thought in your prepared testimony you made an excellent point as to how we should honor the fact that the North Koreans themselves, whether they be in country or in South Korea or anywhere else, are really making the difference and we need to get behind them as never before in those efforts. Maybe you might want to elaborate on that.

Ms. SCHOLTE. Well, why don't I show them the portrait? They smuggled it back in. They smuggled it back into the hearing.

This is an example, okay. Once again, this was made in Pyongyang. This is the response to messages broadcast on Free North Korea Radio, smuggled out at great risk. Two brothers took 3 months to make this.

If they had been caught making this, they and their families would have been executed. So this is just a testament to the importance of reaching out to the people of North Korea.

Mr. SMITH. Thank you.

And what Ms. Scholte is not saying is that there is a portrait of herself and one of Chairman Ed Royce as well.

Is there anything else you would like to add before we conclude? And again, thank you for your insights. It gives us a lot of actionable things to do and I always appreciate that.

Mr. KING. Thank you for this hearing.

Mr. SMITH. Thank you, Ambassador King.

Mr. SCARLATOIU. Thank you for the hearing. Thank you for your dedication and the inspiration that you provide to all of us.

Mr. SMITH. You inspire us. Believe me.

And Ms. Scholte, thank you.

Ms. SCHOLTE. Thank you.

Mr. SMITH. The hearing is adjourned.

[Whereupon, at 4:41 p.m., the committee was adjourned.]

APPENDIX

MATERIAL SUBMITTED FOR THE RECORD

SUBCOMMITTEE HEARING NOTICE
COMMITTEE ON FOREIGN AFFAIRS
U.S. HOUSE OF REPRESENTATIVES
WASHINGTON, DC 20515-6128

Subcommittee on Africa, Global Health, Global Human Rights, and International Organizations
Christopher H. Smith (R-NJ), Chairman

December 8, 2017

TO: MEMBERS OF THE COMMITTEE ON FOREIGN AFFAIRS

You are respectfully requested to attend an OPEN hearing of the Committee on Foreign Affairs, to be held by the Subcommittee Africa, Global Health, Global Human Rights, and International Organizations in Room 2200 of the Rayburn House Office Building (and available live on the Committee website at http://www.ForeignAffairs.house.gov):

DATE: Tuesday, December 12, 2017

TIME: 2:00 p.m.

SUBJECT: Protecting North Korean Refugees

WITNESSES: **Panel I**
Ms. Hyeona Ji
North Korean Defector
Co-chairperson
Worldwide Coalition to Stop Genocide in North Korea

Ms. Han Ga Hee (*alias*)
North Korean Defector
Announcer and Sound Engineer
Free North Korea Radio

Panel II
Mr. Greg Scarlatoiu
Executive Director
The Committee for Human Rights in North Korea

The Honorable Robert King
Senior Adviser
Korea Chair
Center for Strategic and International Studies
(*Former U.S. Special Envoy for North Korean Human Rights Issues*)

Ms. Suzanne Scholte
President
Defense Forum Foundation
Chairwoman
North Korea Freedom Coalition

By Direction of the Chairman

The Committee on Foreign Affairs seeks to make its facilities accessible to persons with disabilities. If you are in need of special accommodations, please call 202/225-5021 at least four business days in advance of the event, whenever practicable. Questions with regard to special accommodations in general (including availability of Committee materials in alternative formats and assistive listening devices) may be directed to the Committee.

COMMITTEE ON FOREIGN AFFAIRS

MINUTES OF SUBCOMMITTEE ON _Africa, Global Health, Global Human Rights, and International Organizations_ HEARING

Day____*Tuesday*____Date____*12/12/17*____Room____*2200*____

Starting Time ____*2:00pm*____ Ending Time ____*4:39pm*____

Recesses [____] (____to____) (____to____) (____to____) (____to____) (____to____) (____to____)

Presiding Member(s)

Smith, Donovan

Check all of the following that apply:

Open Session ☑
Executive (closed) Session ☐
Televised ☐

Electronically Recorded (taped) ☐
Stenographic Record ☑

TITLE OF HEARING:

Protecting North Korean Refugees

SUBCOMMITTEE MEMBERS PRESENT:

Donovan, Bass, Castro

NON-SUBCOMMITTEE MEMBERS PRESENT: *(Mark with an * if they are not members of full committee.)*

HEARING WITNESSES: Same as meeting notice attached? Yes ☑ No ☐
(If "no", please list below and include title, agency, department, or organization.)

STATEMENTS FOR THE RECORD: *(List any statements submitted for the record.)*

-Bass: Written statement by Roberta Cohen, co-chair Emeritus, Committee on Human Rights in North Korea

TIME SCHEDULED TO RECONVENE __________
or
TIME ADJOURNED __________

____
Subcommittee Staff Associate

MATERIAL SUBMITTED FOR THE RECORD BY THE HONORABLE KAREN BASS, A
REPRESENTATIVE IN CONGRESS FROM THE STATE OF CALIFORNIA

WRITTEN STATEMENT OF ROBERTA COHEN, CO-CHAIR EMERITUS, COMMITTEE FOR HUMAN RIGHTS IN NORTH KOREA (HRNK) ON "PROTECTING NORTH KOREAN REFUGEES" AT THE HEARING OF THE SUBCOMMITTEE ON AFRICA, GLOBAL HEALTH, GLOBAL HUMAN RIGHTS, AND INTERNATIONAL ORGANIZATIONS, DECEMBER 12, 2017

My appreciation to Congressman Christopher Smith and Ranking Member Karen Bass for holding this hearing to maintain a spotlight on North Korean refugees and their need for international protection. The world community's preoccupation with massive movements of people fleeing war-torn countries has often overlooked the plight of smaller groups of refugees in desperate straits. The North Korean case is one such situation that should warrant international attention because of the extraordinary cruelty to which the asylum seekers and refugees are subjected. Unlike most governments, North Korea has made it a criminal offense to leave its country without permission, thereby preventing its citizens from exercising their internationally recognized right to seek asylum and become a refugee. Second, those who do try to escape face increasing obstacles -- electrified fences, enhanced border patrols, exorbitant bribes, and traffickers. Only 1,418 managed to reach South Korea in 2016. Third, if caught and returned, North Korean refugees are subject to systematic and brutal punishment, which the United Nations Commission of Inquiry (COI) has found to constitute crimes against humanity.[1] Fourth, neighboring China collaborates with the DPRK in arresting and turning back North Koreans despite the abusive treatment they routinely suffer at the hands of North Korea's security forces.[2]

In his 2017 report to the UN General Assembly, the Special Rapporteur on human rights in the DPRK, Tomas Ojea Quintana, drew attention to the "deplorable conditions" in the holding centers near the border with China where repatriated North Koreans are confined before being sent off to reeducation or other camps for extended punishment. Women constitute the majority of those who flee and of those returned and are "the target of violent practices."[3] During interrogation and detention, they are subject to beatings, torture, and sexual and gender-based violence. Those found to be pregnant are reported to have their pregnancy terminated by force, but "the shame and secrecy attached to this practice make precise statistics on cases of forced abortion difficult to collect."[4] When placed in reeducation through labor camps and other prison facilities, forcibly repatriated North Koreans are deliberately denied adequate food and medical attention, and are subject to forced labor and sexually abusive treatment.

To North Korea, those who leave without permission are criminal offenders, even traitors to the Kim regime. To United Nations human rights bodies, North Koreans who leave illegally are potential refugees. They flee persecution as well as the socioeconomic deprivation emanating

---

[1] UN General Assembly, Report of the commission of inquiry on human rights in the DPRK, A/HRC/25/63, 7 February 2014, paras. 42,76, 89(m) [henceforth COI report].

[2] COI report, ibid., para. 43.

[3] UN General Assembly, Report of the Special Rapporteur on human rights in the DPRK, A/72/394, 19 September 2017, para. 25 [henceforth SR Report].

[4] SR Report, ibid.

from the *songbun* system of social and political classification to which the government subjects them. But even if they were not refugees when they left North Korea, they become so (that is, *refugees sur place*) because of the well-founded fear of persecution and punishment they face upon return. The UN Committee on the Elimination of Discrimination against Women (CEDAW) in 2017 called on North Korea to decriminalize illegal border crossing, and because of the high number of women forcibly repatriated, to ensure that the women "are not subjected to invasive body searches, sexual violence and forced abortions, and that their rights to life and to a fair trial are respected."[5] It further called upon North Korea to allow international organizations "access to all women's detention facilities."[6]

UN bodies have also sent warnings to China, which the UN COI found to be enabling North Korea's crimes. A letter signed by COI Chair, Justice Michael Kirby, and appended to its 400-page report, warned Chinese officials that they could be found to be "aiding and abetting crimes against humanity" by sharing information with North Korea's security bodies and turning back North Koreans to conditions of danger.[7] It challenged China's claims that North Koreans entering China illegally are economic migrants who must be deported, and that those returned are not subject to punishment.

On occasion China has allowed North Koreans to proceed to South Korea, but these cases are few and far between.[8] Over the years China has tolerated thousands of North Koreans residing illegally in its country, some 'married' to Chinese men, but the North Koreans have no rights, are vulnerable to exploitation and bribes, constantly fear deportation and may be expelled. The UN Committee against Torture (CAT) in 2016 described China as practicing a "rigorous policy of forcibly repatriating all nationals of the DPRK" on the grounds that they cross the border illegally for economic reasons.[9] It called on China to set up a refugee determination process for North Koreans and allow UNHCR access to border areas. The CAT noted that it had 100 testimonies showing that North Koreans forcibly returned were "systematically" subjected to torture and ill-treatment and recommended UNHCR monitoring of North Koreans forcibly returned to assure that they are not subject to torture.

When UN Secretary-General Antonio Guterres visited China in 2006 as UN High Commissioner for Refugees, he told Chinese officials that forcibly repatriating North Koreans without any determination process and where they could be persecuted on return stands in violation of the Refugee Convention. UNHCR also proposed a special humanitarian status for North Koreans to enable them to obtain temporary documentation, access to services and protection from

---

[5] UN Committee on the Elimination of Discrimination against Women, Concluding Observations, CEDAW/C/PRK/CO/2-4, 17 November 2017, para. 45 (c).

[6] Ibid., para. 45 (d).

[7] UN General Assembly, Report of the detailed findings of the commission of inquiry on human rights in the DPRK, A/HRC/25/CRP.1, 7 February 2014, para. 1197 [henceforth COI report 2].

[8] See Roberta Cohen, "China's Forced Repatriation of North Korean Refugees Incurs United Nations Censure," *International Journal of Korean Studies*, Spring/Summer 2014, pp. 72-3.

[9] UN Committee against Torture, CAT/C/CHN/CO/5, 3 February 2016, paras. 46-48.

forced return. To the refugee agency, North Koreans are deemed "persons of concern," meriting humanitarian protection.

To date, there has been little progress in persuading North Korea or China to cooperate with the international community. Nonetheless, China's more critical stance toward North Korea of late as well as reports of its making refugee contingency plans in the event of a crisis in North Korea,[10] might lead to more open discussions, the relaxing of some of its policies and the possible modification of others.

The following recommendations are offered with a view to promoting protection for North Korean refugees.

RECOMMENDATIONS
First, an overall international strategy is needed for dealing with the refugee issue. To this end, the United States should propose a *multilateral* approach to the North Korean refugee situation. Just as international burden sharing has been introduced for other refugee populations, so should it be developed here. The North Korean refugee situation is not an economic migrant question for China and North Korea to decide alone according to their own agreements. Other countries are profoundly affected, in particular South Korea whose Constitution offers citizenship to North Koreans and already houses more than 31,000 North Koreans who have fled over the past two decades. Countries in East, Southeast and Central Asia, East and West Europe, and North America have admitted thousands upon thousands, of North Korean refugees. Working together with UNHCR, a multilateral approach could be designed based on principles of *non-refoulement* and human rights protection. Secretary-General Antonio Guterres, who has extensive experience with this and other refugee situations, should be asked to initiate the process.

Second, the United States, South Korea and allied governments should make China's treatment of North Korean refugees a high priority in their *bilateral* dialogues with China. They should make known their willingness to admit North Koreans who cross the border without permission and should call on China to allow UNHCR to begin a determination process so that North Koreans could apply for refugee status and remain temporarily in China while their requests are being processed. The United States and its allies should remind China that more than 150 governments in the General Assembly have called upon China as a country neighboring North Korea to cease the deportation of North Koreans because of the terrible mistreatment they endure upon return. Chinese officials should be encouraged to build on the instances where China has allowed North Koreans to leave for the South, increase such cases and introduce a moratorium on forced repatriations on humanitarian grounds to remain in effect until such time as North Korea ceases its persecution and punishment of those repatriated. A new approach would enhance China's international standing, encourage other states in Asia to uphold international norms, and exert influence on North Korea to modify its practices. China

---

[10] See Jane Perlez, "China Girds for North Korean Refugees," *New York Times*, December 12, 2017; and David E. Sanger, "Tillerson Speaks on a Largely Secret North Korea Contingency Plan," *New York Times*, December 18, 2017.

for its part will need to be assured that the United States and other countries are not seeking to forcibly reunify Korea, destabilize the North and expand United States influence. Certainly, the most effective way to reduce the number of North Koreans going into China is not for the Chinese and North Koreans to push back North Koreans but for the DPRK to begin to provide for the well-being and security of its population.

Third, the United States should expand its practice of identifying and sanctioning North Korean as well as Chinese officials and offices involved in forced repatriations and make them aware that they could be held accountable in future trials. [11] Special Rapporteur Ojea Quintana recently observed that "The more the international community has insisted on the necessity to seek justice…, the more the [North Korean] authorities have seemingly opened to a conversation with human rights mechanisms on ways to fulfil their obligations…"[12] In response to North Koreans' fear of accountability, he described reports, albeit unconfirmed, of improved practices in detention facilities, including toward pregnant women.[13] North Korea also responded for the first time to a United Nations human rights inquiry about returned refugees by providing some statistics. It claimed that only 33 North Korean women out of 6,452 returned from 2005 to 2016 had been punished.[14] This small number of course contradicted the findings of many UN-commissioned reports that spoke of the routine punishment of tens of thousands returned. But North Korea's engagement in the conversation shows that international demarches have had some effect. It is important therefore for the United States to strongly support the collection of evidence about forcibly returned North Koreans and make sure that the Seoul office of the UN High Commissioner for Human Rights (OHCHR), which is tasked with documenting information with a view to accountability, has sufficient resources and staff to perform its functions effectively. In particular, the United States should contribute to the hiring of international criminal justice experts to review existing evidence, including on forced repatriations, and to promote the effective working of a central information and evidence repository to be set up in 2018 to facilitate future prosecutions. It should contribute the names and information it has collected to the central repository.

Fourth, the United States should call on the international humanitarian organizations it funds to request, when appropriate, international access to detention facilities and reeducation camps that house political prisoners, among these, significant numbers of forcibly repatriated women. Such an opportunity arose in September 2016 when a typhoon struck the northeast and flooded not only schools, clinics, roads and agricultural lands, but also a reeducation through labor camp, *Kyo-hwa-so Number 12*, housing some 5,000 prisoners, including up to 1,000

---

[11] In October 2017, the Department of the Treasury announced sanctions on seven North Korean individuals and three entities for hunting down of asylum seekers abroad and other abuses. See "U.S. Sanctions North Koreans for 'Flagrant' Rights Abuse, Reuters, October 26, 2017.

[12] SR Report, para. 3.

[13] SR Report, ibid., para. 26; see also Cohen, "China's Forced Repatriation of North Korean Refugees," pp. 74-75.

[14] North Korea told this to the UN Committee on the Elimination of Discrimination against Women (CEDAW) in 2017. See Elizabeth Shim, "North Korea: Repatriated women defectors are not punished," UPI, August 4, 2017.

forcibly repatriated women.[15] HRNK provided the UN with satellite imagery of the flooded camp, which the Secretary-General included in his report to the General Assembly,[16] but the humanitarian agencies did not try to help the persons inside. It appeared they were reluctant to antagonize North Korean officials and possibly undermine humanitarian operations for other flood victims, despite the fact that information was available to them showing that the women and other prisoners in the camp were given starvation rations, lacked medical care and were subject to exploitation and forced labor.[17] The humanitarian organizations, it should be noted, had some leverage in this case because North Korea had requested the aid and had to listen to their views. While North Korea could have turned down the request, at least the question of entering a flooded camp and reaching its vulnerable people would have been on the table as a legitimate 'ask' to be revisited in future.

It is important that the United States make known to the World Food Program, UNICEF and other humanitarian agencies that they must stand up for *all* people at risk, not just those North Korea might choose to assist, and use the leverage they have to generate meaningful dialogue on the human rights principles central to humanitarian work. Failure to do so will condone the Kim regime's persecution and marginalization of the people it considers disloyal, contrary to the principles upon which humanitarian organizations are founded. Building upon General Assembly resolutions that call on North Korea to grant unimpeded humanitarian access to all affected persons, including those in detention facilities and prisons,[18] the United States should reinforce the recent call made by the UN Special Rapporteur to humanitarian agencies: he said they should "ensure" that their programs benefit "vulnerable groups, including those who are in detention facilities, prison camps and political prison camps."[19] It is also time for the United States to urge Secretary-General Guterres to apply to North Korea the UN policy of 2013 which he endorsed — namely the Human Rights up Front (HRuF) approach, which calls upon the entire UN system to come together in the face of serious human rights violations and take steps on behalf of the victims.

Fifth, the United States should develop contingency plans with China for addressing a crisis in the north that also encompasses protection and assistance for refugees and internally displaced persons (IDPs). Significant numbers of North Koreans can be expected to flee to China and South Korea in the event of an emergency, and even more become internally displaced, making it desirable for the United States and South Korea to develop plans with China for managing migration.[20] China is already reported to be constructing refugee camps along its border areas

---

[15] Roberta Cohen, "UN Humanitarian Actors and North Korea's Prison Camps," *International Journal of Korean Studies*, Spring/Summer 2017, pp. 1-24.

[16] UN General Assembly, Report of the Secretary-General on the situation of human rights in the DPRK, A/72/279, 3 August 2017, para. 37.

[17] COI report 2, para. 804.

[18] UN General Assembly, Resolution on the Situation of human rights in the DPRK, A/C.3/72/L.40, 31 October 2017, paras. 2(vi), 5, and 15(m).

[19] SR Report, para. 48.

[20] See Roberta Cohen, "Human Rights and Humanitarian Planning for Crisis in North Korea," *International Journal of Korean Studies*, Fall/Winter 2015, pp. 11-16.

with North Korea.[21] An agreement among the three under United Nations auspices should aim at stabilization of the peninsula, provision of material aid, protection of displaced persons, and incentives and opportunities to build and transform the country in accordance with international human rights, humanitarian and refugee standards and humane treatment of displaced persons.

Finally, the United States should revisit any restrictions now placed on the admission of North Korean refugees that could conflict with the spirit and intent of the North Korean Human Rights Act (2004). Our government should make known its readiness, given the persecution and punishment to which North Koreans are subject, to increase the number of North Korean refugees admitted to this country. In FY 2017, only 12 were reported to be admitted, contributing to a total of 212 since 2006. While the vast majority of North Koreans will choose to seek refuge in South Korea, some have reasons for seeking to resettle in the United States, and should not be discouraged. As Victor Cha and Robert Gallucci have recommended the United States should "seek public and private sector funding" for "educational scholarships and vocational training," [22] in particular from the Korean American community, to empower the North Koreans already admitted to this country and help them overcome the traumas they experienced in fleeing one of the most tyrannical governments on the planet.

---

[21] See Jane Perlez, "China Girds for North Korean Refugees," *New York Times*, December 12, 2017; and "Report: China's Military Prepared for Collapse Scenario," *Daily NK*, May 5, 2014.

[22] See Victor Cha and Robert L. Gallucci, *Toward a New Policy and Strategy for North Korea*, George W. Bush Institute, 2016, p. 8; and *Education and Employment Among U.S.-Based North Koreans: Challenges and Opportunities*, George W. Bush Institute, 2016.

www.ingramcontent.com/pod-product-compliance
Lightning Source LLC
Chambersburg PA
CBHW081846250726
48659CB00008B/2634